EVOLUTION
IS LOVE
IN ACTION

EVOLUTION IS LOVE IN ACTION

YOU ARE CALLED TO BE THE EVOLUTION OF LOVE

AWAKENING TO THE ALLUREMENT THAT GUIDES THE UNIVERSE

• • •

*From Conscious Evolution 1.0
to Conscious Evolution 2.0*

*One Mountain, Many Paths: Oral Essays
Volume Eight*

DR. MARC GAFNI AND
BARBARA MARX HUBBARD

Author: Marc Gafni and Barbara Marx Hubbard
Title: Evolution Is Love in Action
From Conscious Evolution 1.0 to Conscious Evolution 2.0

Identifiers: ISBN 979-8-88834-076-9 (electronic)
ISBN 979-8–88834–075–2 (paperback)

Edited by Timothy Paul Aryeh, Paul Bennett, David Cicerchi, and Terry Nelson

World Philosophy and Religion Press, St. Johnsbury, VT
in conjunction with

IP Integral Publishers

https://worldphilosophyandreligion.org

JOIN THE REVOLUTION!

CONTENTS

EDITORIAL NOTE ABOUT AUTHORSHIP, EDITING, AND THE RADICAL CONTEXT FOR THIS SERIES

ORAL ESSAYS FROM THE ONE MOUNTAIN, MANY PATHS WEEKLY BROADCAST

This volume is part of the Oral Essays library, a series of lightly edited, compiled transcripts of oral teachings given by Dr. Marc Gafni and the late Barbara Marx Hubbard in their weekly online broadcast, *One Mountain, Many Paths,* which they co-founded in 2017. Originally called an "Evolutionary Church," *One Mountain, Many Paths* became a key venue for the articulation of an inspired and deeply grounded new Story of Value in response to the meta-crisis. Marc and Barbara—together with Zak Stein,[1] Kristina Kincaid, Ken Wilber, Sally Kempton, Lori Galperin, Aubrey Marcus and dozens of other thought-leaders over the years—began to articulate what they call a World Philosophy and World Religion[2] as a context for our diversity.

---

1   Zak, together with Ken Wilber, has been Marc's primary intellectual partner and an initiate lineage holder in CosmoErotic Humanism.

2   This project is grounded in four core organizational frameworks: 1) The Center for World Philosophy and Religion, co-founded by Marc Gafni, Zachary Stein, Sally Kempton, and Ken Wilber, and chaired over the years by John P. Mackey, Barbara Marx Hubbard, Aubrey Marcus, Gabrielle Anwar and Shareef Malnik, Carrie Kish and Adam Bellow, and Kathleen J. Brownback. 2) The Office for the Future, chaired by Stephanie Valcke and Ivan Bossyut. 3) The World Philosophy and Religion Press, founded and chaired by Aubrey Marcus, together with Marc Gafni and Zachary Stein. 4) The Foundation for Conscious Evolution, founded by Barbara Marx Hubbard and currently chaired by Peter Fiekowsky. For a complete list of key leadership, see the Office for the Future website, www.officeforthefuture.com.

Until Barbara's passing in 2019, she and Marc transmitted teachings together as evolutionary partners and "whole mates," weaving together insights and transmissions from their decades of practice, study, teaching, and activism into a synergy of wisdom, a grounded vision for future policy across all sectors of society.

Much of the Dharma material below comes directly from Marc, so it was originally all in quotation marks—but that looked a little odd. So per his suggestion we removed them, and the reader should consider the paragraphs on the next several pages as one extended quote from him. We are joyfully grateful to Marc for the clarity of his Dharma, the elegance and "second simplicity" of this language, and the mad, Outrageous Love with which he transmits his teachings.

Barbara and Marc called the mission of *One Mountain* "a Planetary Awakening in Evolutionary Love Through Unique Self Symphonies." We are an evolutionary community with a deeply grounded, radically alive, and "post-tragic" revolutionary spirit. We are activating a new humanity and awakening as a new species: *Homo amor*, the fulfillment of *Homo sapiens*.

One Mountain is committed to articulating a Story of Value that can become the ground for the new society that must be birthed in response to the meta-crisis. We recognize that we are living at a pivotal moment in history. In this "time between stories," the great moral imperative is to tell the new Story of Value. It is ours to do, personally and collectively, with great trembling and ecstatic joy.

FROM DOGMA TO DHARMA: ETERNAL AND EVOLVING FIRST PRINCIPLES AND FIRST VALUES

The teachings are grounded in decades of deep study across many wisdom traditions. Over the years, week by week, these teachings were incrementally developed within the framework of the *One Mountain, Many Paths* broadcast. We often refer to these teachings as *Dharma*.

This word was originally used in lineage traditions to refer to something like universal law. This is a crucial realization: just as there is universal law in mathematical value, there is also a sense of universal law in ethics and value.

Historically, Dharma often devolved into unchanging dogma. Evolution was ignored, and the natural process of Dharma evolution became disconnected from its deep, eternal context. The weakness of the word Dharma is that too often it did not include the evolving insights of the sciences, it confused local cultural truths with universal truths, and it used words like "eternal," as in "eternal Tao," as opposed to words like "evolution."

Eternal came to mean unchanging, and that kind of thinking often led to overly ethnocentric readings of Dharma. Local systems would claim their religious and cultural insights as immutable, which stood in the way of the emergence of a genuine world Story of Value that is real, inherent to Cosmos, and backed by the Universe—even as it is also always evolving.

Or, as we often say, "eternal value is evolving value. The eternal Tao is the evolving Tao."

We have shown that, emergent from profound insights in the "interior sciences," eternal does not mean unchanging in time; it means what we call the deeper Field of ErosValue that is beneath culture, geography, and history, which lives beneath all individual and collective values, and beneath time and space itself.

As such, we have gradually transitioned from the term Dharma to the term *Value*, in the sense of the Field of Value that lives beneath all values. This Field of Value discloses as First Principles and First Values embedded in a Story of Value.

Indeed, as the interior sciences knew and the exterior sciences imply, Reality arises in a Field of ErosValue in which an entire set of mathematical, musical, molecular, moral, and mystical values are the very ground of all being. That Field of Value is eternal—the true ground of the Good, True and Beautiful—even as it is evolving.

But of course, it is equally critical not just to talk about evolving value, but to ground the evolving value in its true nature, the eternal Field of First Principles and First Values, always reaching for ever-more life, ever-more love, ever-more care, ever-more depth, ever-more uniqueness, ever-more intimate communion, and ever-more transformation.

As such, when we refer to the word Dharma, which still appears in these texts together with the word value, we refer to an evolving Dharma grounded in an *eternal and evolving* Field of Value. Indeed, eternity and evolution are two faces of the whole, opposites joined at the hip, that characterize the nature of our Cosmos in virtually all of its expressions.

It's in these terms that we ground a robust world philosophy that integrates the validated, leading-edge insights of premodern traditional wisdom, modern wisdom, and more recent postmodern insights, weaving them together into a new whole greater than the sum of its parts.

This new whole is a shared Story of Value rooted in First Principles and First Values that are both eternal and evolving.

These First Principles and First Values of Cosmos are woven together into a new Story of Value as a context for our diversity, a new Universe Story. This new Story gives us the best possible responses we have to the mystery, and to the great questions:

- Who am I? Who are we?
- Where am I? Where are we?
- What should I do? What should we do?

It is only through such a shared Universe Story—a narrative of identity and ethos as a context for our blessed diversity—that we can realize how what unites is so much greater than what divides us.

Only a new Story of Value will allow us to both respond to the meta-crisis and participate together in birthing the most true, good, and beautiful world that we already know is possible.

THIS ORAL ESSAYS SERIES IS AN ENTRYWAY TO THE GREAT LIBRARY OF COSMOEROTIC HUMANISM

This Oral Essays series is part of the overarching project of the Great Library at the Center for World Philosophy and Religion, led by Dr. Marc Gafni, together with Dr. Zak Stein. The aim of the Great Library project is to articulate a robust and comprehensive new Story of Value, CosmoErotic Humanism, in the form of dozens of well-researched and extensively footnoted academic works.

Our vision is to provide the philosophical framework that will be vital for navigating humanity through this time of immense crisis and transformation.

To begin your journey into CosmoErotic Humanism, we tenderly refer you to the book *First Principles and First Values*, co-authored by Marc Gafni, Zak Stein, and Ken Wilber, under the name David J. Temple. David J. Temple is a pseudonym created for enabling ongoing collaborative authorship at the Center for World Philosophy and Religion. The two primary authors behind David J. Temple are Marc Gafni and Zak Stein, and for different projects, specific writers will be named as part of the collaboration, such as Ken Wilber and others.

Three other volumes complete this introduction: *A Return to Eros*, by Marc Gafni and Kristina Kincaid; *Your Unique Self*, by Marc Gafni; and *Education in a Time between Worlds*, by Zak Stein.

We hope that the Oral Essays in this volume, with their informal style of transmission, will serve as an allurement and entryway for you into the more formal books of the Great Library that provide the robust intellectual underpinnings of the new Story of Value.

A NOTE ABOUT THE EDITORS

This Oral Essays collection has been edited by students of the new Story of CosmoErotic Humanism. Each of us has actively participated in *One Mountain, Many Paths*, and most of us have been in deep "Holy of Holies" study with Dr. Marc Gafni for many years.

We have been privileged to find ourselves well-versed in the teachings, and even emerging as lineage-holders of CosmoErotic Humanism.[3]

We view this editing project as a privilege and a deep practice of study and clarification. We experience ourselves as a *mystical editing society*, frequently meeting and conversing together about the content—the depth of knowledge and wisdom offered here—as well as the technical intricacies involved with publishing a beautiful and coherent series of books. In so doing, we function as a "Unique Self Symphony," which itself is a Dharmic

---

3 CosmoErotic Humanism is a world philosophical movement aimed at reconstructing the collapse of value at the core of global culture. Much like Romanticism or Existentialism, CosmoErotic Humanism is not merely a theory but a movement that changes the very mood of Reality. It is an invitation to participate in evolving the source code of consciousness and culture towards a cosmocentric *ethos* for a planetary civilization.

The term CosmoErotic Humanism, initially coined by Dr. Gafni and colleagues, points to a complex, multi-faceted, layered, and nuanced evolutionary set of insights that has evolved over decades of intensive research, teaching, and spiritual practice from deep within a wide range of wisdom traditions (including the Wisdom of Solomon lineage tradition, Bodhisattva Buddhism, and Kashmir Shaivism), as well as multiple disciplines including complexity theory, chaos theory, emergence theory, molecular biology, and the more classical disciplines of the humanities.

The seeds of CosmoErotic Humanism were planted with Dr. Marc Gafni's work on a two-volume, 1,000-page opus called *Radical Kabbalah* (Integral Publishers, 2012). This scholarly work, sourced from deep study within the esoteric lineage texts of the Wisdom of Solomon, points to a non-dual, or acosmic, realization which—unlike the prevailing conceptualization of non-duality—does not efface the human being; rather, it is highly humanistic in its nature. The next step in the evolution of CosmoErotic Humanism was the insight that all of Reality is evolving Eros, which lives in, as, and through the human being.

A failure of Eros leads inexorably to the creation of narratives of "pseudo-eros." CosmoErotic Humanism is a response to the modern mental and social breakdown sourced in the proliferation of multiple forms of pseudo-eros and its broken narratives, such as rivalrous conflict governed by win/lose metrics and the dogmatic denial of intrinsic value in Cosmos, which together generate our current "global intimacy disorder."

term that connotes an omni-considerate collaboration between realized Unique Selves synergizing our unique gifts into a new emergence greater than the sum of the parts. Even as we worked diligently to standardize our editing styles, meeting on a weekly basis to debate the nuances of phrasing, we also operated from within a deep appreciation of the unique style that each editor brought to his or her work. As such, the reader might notice some variation in editing style among the books.

Please note that Dr. Marc Gafni has not reviewed these edited Oral Essays, as he is deeply engaged in writing the formal books of the Great Library. But he has been generous in responding to questions and providing overall guidance in the project. Overall, as Marc's students and students of the Dharma, we have made it a key project at the Center to publish these pieces of work relatively independently.

OUR UNIQUE ORAL-ESSAY EDITING STYLE PRESERVES THE ENERGY OF THE ORIGINAL TRANSMISSION

Dr. Marc Gafni is a uniquely gifted teacher whose oral transmission is imbued with a quality that has proven transformative for his students. Many of us feel mystically transformed by both the content and the underlying energy of the transmission style. Therefore, as we like to say, *trust the magic ways the Dharma comes through your unique understanding!*

As Marc's empowered students, colleagues, and Beloved friends, we have a deep knowing that these teachings are vital for the survival and thriving of humanity as we know it, and we recognize the importance of publishing his teachings in a written format that will be accessible by future generations.

At the same time, we sought to preserve the Eros of the original oral transmission with all of its nuance, power, and depth.

Our intention in the editing process, to the greatest extent possible, has been to keep these spoken artifacts intact in order to maintain the flow of the original transmission. We have therefore chosen not to engage in intensive formal editing, as we found that doing so resulted in the loss of the energetic transmission that is so key to fully receiving the Dharma.

After experimenting with many ways to present these texts, we developed a specific way of laying out the text on the page. Marc, in collaboration with Zak Stein and Russian intellectual/artist Elena Maslova-Levin—and ultimately all of the editors, through many conversations—developed a unique, artistic presentation of the text, using bolding, italics, bullet points, and other stylistic features which together serve to accentuate the immediacy of the oral transmission.

As part of this editing style, intended to preserve the integrity of the original transmission, we have refrained from removing the frequent recapitulations of key themes. We found that each recapitulation contributes something vital to the rhythm and music beneath the words, like the beating drum of our hearts.

These recapitulations not only review previous material but also add important new emphases, perspectives, and elements of the new Story of Value. We ask for your patience as a reader to trust the rhythm of these texts, and we trust you as a reader to have the depth and steadiness to find your way through.

KEY COMPONENTS: LINK TO THE ORIGINAL BROADCAST, EVOLUTIONARY LOVE CODES AND PRAYER

To supplement the written word, each episode includes a QR code linking to the original broadcast on YouTube, as well as occasional links to featured songs and video clips.

Each episode also centers around an "Evolutionary Love Code," formulated by Marc. These codes are part of the ongoing articulation and distillation of the Dharma as it unfolds and emerges, week by week, over the course of many years, through the mystical process we call Outrageous Love or Evolutionary Love.

Another core component of the *One Mountain, Many Paths* episodes is what Marc and Barbara called "Evolutionary Prayer." Prayer is experienced in *One Mountain* not in the old fundamentalist sense of a "cosmic vending-machine god" who is alienated from Cosmos. Marc refers to this as the "god you do not and should not believe in"—and he often adds, "the god you don't believe in does not exist."

GOD IS THE INFINITE INTIMATE

In fact, in the Dharma of CosmoErotic Humanism, a new name for God has emerged: the "Infinite Intimate," who appears in first-, second-, and third-person expressions. Marc first shared this name as he heard it whispered in 2023, although earlier intimations and formulations of the name appeared as early as 2010.

In first person, God is infinitely alive and as intimate as our own first-person experience.

In second person, God is the infinitely intimate Personhood of Cosmos that knows our name and holds us—the God about whom we say, *whenever we fall, we fall into Her hands.* This is the God who is our Beloved, Father, Mother, Lover, and Evolutionary Partner.

Finally, in third person, God inheres in all of the First Principles and First Values of Cosmos, and in the laws of science (both interior and exterior) that govern manifest Reality.

Therefore, we have a realization of God as not only the Infinity of Power but also the Infinity of Intimacy.

In *One Mountain, Many Paths*, we are reclaiming prayer at a higher level of consciousness. And we are reclaiming prayer as deep, alive, loving, and intimate conversations with God as the Infinite Intimate who knows our name.

REFLECTING ON THE CO-CREATION BETWEEN DR. MARC GAFNI AND BARBARA MARX HUBBARD

Barbara and Marc met five years before Barbara passed. As Barbara said so often, "before I met Marc, I was sure that I was done." Barbara had taught so beautifully for decades, focusing particularly on a powerful articulation of "conscious evolution." Indeed, it would not be inaccurate to say that Barbara was the greatest storyteller of conscious evolution of her time.

Conscious evolution was also a premise in Marc's thinking, but drawn from an entirely different set of sources and experiences. Barbara drew from the classical sources of evolutionary spirituality, such as Teilhard de Chardin, Buckminster Fuller, and many others. Indeed, she was closely associated with Fuller, and was perhaps de Chardin's most ardent intellectual devotee.

Marc drew a somewhat different vision of conscious evolution from the interior sciences of the great wisdom traditions, with a primary emphasis on what he refers to as the "Solomon lineages," merged together with careful readings of the leading edges of the sciences. In the old version of conscious evolution, the movement from unconscious to conscious was a movement of evolution by chance to evolution by choice.

Together Marc and Barbara evolved the old version of Conscious Evolution, pointing out that evolution itself was always in some sense conscious, but as Marc formulated it, the awakening to conscious evolution refers to the awakening of evolution as human consciousness, coupled with the human realization of being conscious evolution in person, and the human capacity to locate oneself within the context of the larger evolutionary story.

Marc focused his attention on an entirely different dimension of Reality, which he and his colleagues began to call CosmoErotic Humanism. The Intimate Universe, Homo amor, Unique Self and Unique Self Symphonies, God as the Infinity of Intimacy, Eros and the CosmoErotic Universe, distinctions like Role Mate, Soul Mate and Whole Mate, the Four Selves, Evolutionary Love, Outrageous Love, Evolution: the Love Story of the Universe, First Principles and First Values, Evolving Perennialism, the Evolution of Love, and many more are terms articulated by Gafni and shared with Barbara in their conversation, study, and creative engagement.

Some terms they coined together, for example "a Planetary Awakening in Love through Unique Self Symphonies," where Gafni described Unique Self Symphonies, and Barbara aligned her vision of a planetary Pentecost to Marc's vision of Unique Self Symphonies.

Other key terms were unique and articulated by Barbara, for example: conscious evolution, teleros, telerotic, from joining genes to joining genius, regenopause, vocational arousal, birthing of humanity, synergy engine, and of course her work around what she called the Wheel of Co-creation.

Ultimately, Marc and Barbara attempted to synergize their work in what they called the Wheel of Co-creation 2.0. Barbara and Marc experienced themselves as merging their respective Dharma into what they began to refer to as Conscious Evolution 2.0, or later, CosmoErotic Humanism.

The first 129 episodes of One Mountain, Many Paths took place in the last period of Barbara's life and reflect the depth and texture of the stunning evolutionary whole-mate meeting between her and Marc.

As Barbara was deep in study with Marc, a lot of what she shared in Evolutionary Church was the Dharma of their deep study and collaboration.

Although sometimes it may be clear who is speaking, we generally publish these early episodes in what we are calling "one voice." The first 129 episodes, with Marc and Barbara together, have been grouped chronologically. Episodes 130 to 400 and onwards, which were transmitted by Marc, have been grouped by topic.

THE INVITATION

We invite you to find your way into this revolution. Each one of our Unique Selves and unique gifts are desperately needed as we co-create this new Story of Value together, as part of the covenant between generations, for the sake of the whole.

Let's *play a larger game* and evolve the very source code of consciousness and culture together.

With mad love,

The Editors

LOVE OR DIE

LOCATING OURSELVES: ARTICULATING THE ESSENTIAL CONTEXT FOR THE ONE MOUNTAIN, MANY PATHS ORAL ESSAYS

SETTING OUR INTENTION

Intention setting is everything.

We're here—as da Vinci was with his cohort in the Renaissance—**to play a larger game, to participate in the evolution of love, which is to tell the new Story of Value rooted in First Principles and First Values.**

- ◆ Our intention is to recognize the critical historical juncture in which we find ourselves.
- ◆ Our intention is to take our seat at the table of history and to say, *we take responsibility for this*.
- ◆ Our intention is to participate as revolutionaries for the sake of the whole.

What we're here to do is revolution; revolution for the sake of the evolution of love.

It's a revolution for the sake of the trillions of unborn lives that will not manifest:

- The unborn loves
- The unborn creativity
- The unborn goodness
- The unborn truth
- The unborn beauty

All of it looks to us.

Not because we're engaged in grandiosity. Not at all!

- We're trembling before She.
- We're trembling with joy at the privilege.
- We're trembling with joy at the responsibility.
- We're trembling with joy at the Possibility of Possibility.
- We have to enact a new Story in this moment of time. Because it is only a new Story that can change the vector of history.

The most revolutionary act that we can do—the greatest moral imperative of this time—**is to articulate a new Story at this time between worlds and this time between stories**.

Story is not made up, as postmodernity suggests. **We all live in inescapable frameworks; our framework is the story we live in.** Right now, Reality lives according to win/lose metrics, a story that is generating existential risk. **We need to change that story.**

When we change that story, when we tell a new Story—not a made-up story, but a new Story of Value, rooted in First Principles and First Values—**then it all changes.**

We need to participate in the evolution of the source code of consciousness and culture, which is the evolution of love.

It's the most important, exciting, evolutionary, revolutionary act that we can do to alleviate suffering: to be lovers.

Like Rumi, the great poet of Sufism, we have to be "mad lovers," because it's the only sanity.

To be mad lovers is to see around the corner, to not be so obsessed with the details of the contractions of my life.

Let me see bigger.

Let me take complete care of myself in every possible way, let me completely attend to those in my circle of intimacy and influence, and then—*let me expand my circle.*

That's what we're here for.

- Our intention is to participate in the *LoveForce*, the *LoveIntelligence*, the *LoveBeauty*, the *LoveDesire* that literally animates Cosmos all the way up and all the way down.
- Our intention is to participate in the evolution of love.

    [In the next few pages we will cover some key concepts which are essential to locating ourselves and setting the context for all the One Mountain, Many Paths Oral Essays. —Eds.]

OVERVIEW: EROS IS NO LONGER A LUXURY—IT'S LOVE OR DIE

Eros is life.

The failure of Eros destroys life.

Our lack of Eros is poised to destroy the world.

All civilizations have fallen because the stories that they lived in were, in some sense, stories based on rivalrous conflict governed by win/lose metrics. Every civilization was weakened by interior polarization caused by the lack of a shared Story of Value.

We now have a global civilization, but we haven't created a shared Story of Value.

We haven't solved the generator functions that caused all civilizations to fall. Our global civilization has exponential technologies and extraction models depleting the Earth of resources that took billions of years to create, which is going to lead to a civilizational collapse.

Existential risk is risk to our very existence.

The choice is clear: love or die.

It's that simple.

Eros is no longer a luxury. It is an absolute necessity for the survival of the individual and the planet.

In the last half a century, modern psychology has documented an age-old truth: a fully nourished baby who is not held in loving arms will die.

So too, our world, both personal and global—even with all the resources of intelligence and technology at our disposal—will die without being held in love, in the embrace of Eros.

We must embrace a personal path of love and a global politics of love.

Not ordinary love. Not love which is "mere human sentiment," but Eros, or what we sometimes call Outrageous Love, which is the heart of existence itself.

We live in a world of outrageous pain.

The only response is Outrageous Love.

WHAT IS EROS?

Eros is the experience of radical aliveness, moving towards, seeking, desiring ever-deeper contact and ever-greater wholeness.[4] Eros is the core fabric of Reality's being and the motivational architecture of Reality's becoming.

Eros is what animates the evolutionary impulse itself, from the very inception of Cosmos all the way to our very selves, who awaken to the realization that the evolutionary impulse throbs uniquely in each of us.

The realization of human awakening and transformation that lies at the core of the interior sciences is the invitation—or even the urgent and desperate demand—of a madly loving Cosmos animated by infinities of power and infinities of intimacy.

The demand—the desperate invitation, the plea, the tender and fierce command of Cosmos that lives inside every human being—is to awaken: to awaken to our true nature as unique incarnations of Eros and Ethos that are needed and desperately desired by All-That-Is. Said slightly differently: Reality is Eros. Or: God is Eros.

The failure of Eros destroys life. The collapse of Eros is always the hidden (or not so hidden) root cause for the collapse of ethics.

This is true both personally and collectively. We live in a moment of a world-wide and personal collapse of Eros. Our lack of Eros is poised to destroy

---

4 We define Eros through what we refer to as the Eros equation (one of a series of what we call interior science equations):

> *Eros = Radical Aliveness* x *Desiring (Growing + Seeking)* x *Deeper Contact* x *Greater Wholeness* x *Self Actualization/Self Transcendence (Creation [Destruction])*

There are good reasons for the formal language of the interior science equations in these writings, and the reader is invited to explore them on their own, in particular, in our work, David J. Temple, *First Principles and First Values: Forty-Two Propositions on CosmoErotic Humanism, the Meta-Crisis, and the World to Come* (World Philosophy and Religion, 2024).

the world. Humanity is currently experiencing what has come to be known as existential risk, a risk to our very existence, or what I will refer to as the Second Shock of Existence.

EXISTENTIAL RISK: THE SECOND SHOCK OF EXISTENCE

The first shock of existence is the death of the human being—the realization that we will die, which dawns in human consciousness at the beginning of history. We are not talking about the biological fact of death but the *existential* realization of death. Although the interior sciences disclose that death is a portal between two days (there is vast empirical,[5] philosophical,[6] and anthro-ontological evidence[7] for the continuity of consciousness[8]), death is also, in our own direct surface experience, a stark end. And that is obviously not a bug but a feature in the system.

---

5   We refer to evidence gathered by the most serious of researchers, beginning with Henry and Edith Sedgwick at Cambridge University and William James at Harvard University, and continuing in highly rigorous form for the last 150 years, as recapitulated by Whiteheadian scholar David Ray Griffin in multiple volumes. See also, for example, Dean Radin, *Real Magic: Unlocking Your Natural Psychic Abilities to Create Everyday Miracles* (Potter/TenSpeed/Harmony, 2018), *The Conscious Universe: The Scientific Truth of Psychic Phenomena* (HarperCollins, 2010), and other books. Or see the earlier classic by Frederic William Henry Myers, *Human Personality and Its Survival of Bodily Death* (Longmans, Green, 1907).

6   This requires a cogent analysis of materialism and dualism, and the introduction of the far more cogent third possibility which we have called "pan-interiority."

7   We discuss Anthro-Ontology in some depth in *First Principles and First Values*, and see also the fuller conversation in David J. Temple, *First Principles and First Values: Towards an Evolving Perennialism: Introducing the Anthro-Ontological Method*—both published by World Philosophy and Religion Press, in Conjunction with Integral Publishers. For now, we will simply define it as an "innate and clear interior gnosis directly available to the human being."

8   See Dr. Marc Gafni and Dr. Zachary Stein's essay in preparation, "Beyond Death: Anthro-Ontology, Philosophy, and Empiricism." This essay is slated to appear in the book *Towards a World Religion: Homo Amor Essays*. The essay is also the ground for a larger book by the same authors, *Twelve Portals to Life Beyond Death: Responding to the Second Shock of Existence,* in which we discuss three forms of material: the empirical, the philosophical, and the anthro-ontological, and show how each form discredits the notion of death as the end.

Our first-person experience is that death ends this life. It is not the *totality* of our experience if we go deeper inside, but it is obviously intended to be the central, potent, and painful dimension of every human life. Indeed, as Ernest Becker potently reminded us, the denial of death is at our peril.

All the stories and all the plotlines and all the threads of living end at that moment. Whatever happens beyond, we have an actual experience of ending. **Paradoxically, that ending, the experience of the finality of mortality, is what presses us into life.** From the implicit demand of the first shock of existence, human beings were activated and pressed into creative emergence, and what emerged was all of human culture, both interior and exterior.

The second shock of existence is the realization of the potential death of all humanity. After all the stages of human history—matter, life, and mind in all of their stages of evolutionary unfolding—we have come to this place in the evolution of humanity, in which the gap between our exponentially expanding exterior technologies and our stalled (or even regressing) interior technologies of value has created dire catastrophic and existential risks.

This gap generates extraction models and exponential growth curves, rivalrous conflicts based on win/lose metrics, tragedies of the commons, and multipolar traps, in which everyone has to keep producing to the *n*th degree, including weaponized exponential threats to our very existence because we are afraid that the other parties are going to do it and not be transparent—hide it from us and then dominate us.

GENERATOR FUNCTIONS FOR EXISTENTIAL RISK

Let's outline clearly the main *generator functions for existential risk*.

Rivalrous conflicts governed by zero-sum, win/lose metrics. Rivalrous conflicts generate extraction models at the core of the economic system and exponential growth curves. Both of these drive and are driven by a contrived system of artificially manufactured desires and needs, delivered into culture by ever more precise forms of micro-targeting to individuals and groups through the ever more immersive environment of the internet.

Next, rivalrous conflicts and exponential growth curves animated by win/lose metrics generate **complicated, fragile world systems** highly vulnerable to myriad forms of collapse. Fragile local systems are made exponentially more fragile on a global level by our inability to meet global challenges with social, legal, political, economic, and ethical infrastructures that remain largely local.

All of this is a direct result of the failure to develop more adequate interior technologies that would be sufficiently compelling to displace "rivalrous conflict governed by win/lose metrics" as the motivational architecture for the human life world.

This failure has led to the conditions that will cause the implosion of systems that are already and quite literally on the brink of collapsing themselves. That's what we mean by the *second shock of existence*.

To recapitulate: the second shock of existence is not the death of the human being, but the potential death of humanity.

It is the *Death Star* moment of our species.

THE DECONSTRUCTION OF INTRINSIC VALUE

We stand in this moment poised between utopia and dystopia, at a time between worlds and a time between stories. We need a new Story of Value, eternal yet evolving, rooted in First Principles and First Values, which would become a universal grammar of value and a context for our diversity.

This is exactly what the Renaissance was. It was a time between worlds and a time between stories. In the Renaissance, we had recently been challenged by the Black Death, a pandemic that swept across Europe. The Black Death destroyed between a third to half of Europe and a huge part of

Asia. People died horrifically, brutally, in the streets. They had no idea how to meet this challenge, and so, in response to the Black Death, da Vinci and Ficino and their cohorts understood that they had to tell a new Story of Value.

That story was the story of modernity. Did they get it right?

- They got part of it right, which birthed, to use Jürgen Habermas' phrase, "the dignities of modernity," such as new ways of gathering information and universal human rights.
- But they also deconstructed the source of Value. They lost the basis for the Good, the True, and the Beautiful.

The basis used to be divine revelation: *God told us.* But this claim was owned by religion, and every religion began to overreach and over-claim. The revelation was thus often mediated through cultural categories and wasn't fully accurate.

> *Modernity threw out revelation, but was unable to establish a new basis for value.*

Value was just assumed to be real. As it says in the founding document of the American Revolution: *We hold these truths to be self-evident*—that is, *we don't really have a basis for value; we just take it as a given.*

In other words, modernity took out a loan of social capital from the traditional world. The source of value was never worked out.

And then, gradually, value began to collapse.

- The Universe Story began to collapse.
- The belief that the Good, the True, and the Beautiful are real began to collapse.
- The belief that Love is real began to collapse.

As Bertrand Russell is reported to have said, "I cannot see how to refute the arguments for the subjectivity of ethical values, but I find myself incapable of believing that all that is wrong with wanton cruelty is that I do not like it."

What do you do if you grew up in a world in which value is not real? A world without a source of value, without a Universe Story, without a story of human identity, without a story of desire, without a narrative of power?

In the words of W.B. Yeats, *the center does not hold.*

- You have a collapse at the very center of society, because you no longer have Eros.
- You no longer have a Reality in which value is real, and so you have this lingering sense of emptiness.
- You have a complete collapse at the very center.
- We become *the hollow men and the stuffed men*, gesture without form.

And that's the source of our current existential risk.

THE DEEPER ROOT CAUSE OF THE META-CRISIS: A GLOBAL INTIMACY DISORDER

Above, I have outlined the major generator functions of existential risk. But there is a deeper cause for the existential risk that lurks underneath the rivalrous conflict governed by win/lose metrics and the fragile systems they engender.

And we cannot take the Death Star down without discerning and addressing this. We have already alluded to this root cause above, but at this point we need to make it more explicit so that, from this context, the adequate root response will become clear.

Modernity threw out the revelation, but was unable to establish a new basis for value.

This ostensibly surprising statement can be understood in a few simple steps:

1. All of the catastrophic and existential risk challenges we face are global: from climate change to artificial intelligence, pandemics, systems collapse, and exponential arms races.
2. Every global challenge self-evidently requires a global solution.
3. Global solutions can only be implemented with global co-ordination.
4. Global co-ordination is impossible without global coherence.
5. Global coherence is only possible if there is a global resonance between the parts.
6. Global resonance is only possible if we have global intimacy.

ONLY A SHARED STORY OF VALUE CAN GENERATE GLOBAL INTIMACY

Global intimacy—just like intimacy in a couple—is only possible when there is a shared story.

Not just a shared history, but a shared Story of Value.

- It is only a shared global story that can generate a new emergent quality of intimacy: global intimacy.
- A shared Story of Value must be rooted in shared ordinating values, or what we have called evolving First Values and First Principles.
- Intimacy requires a shared grammar of value as a matrix for a shared Story of Value.

The global intimacy disorder is the root cause for existential risk. The global intimacy disorder underlies the core generator functions for existential risk.

The global intimacy disorder is rooted in the failure to experience ourselves in a field of shared intrinsic value. This failure derives from the deconstruction of value.

Indeed, it is wholly accurate to say that **the root cause of the two generator functions of existential risk is the failed story of intrinsic value, or what we might also call the breakdown of Eros**.

1. The first generator function is **the success story**. Our modern success story is rivalrous conflict governed by win/lose metrics, which violates all the terms of the Intimacy Equation: there is no shared identity and no mutuality of recognition, feeling, value or purpose, and instead of *relative* otherness, there is *alienated* otherness. Such a story generates complicated fragile systems with no allurement or intimacy between the parts, systems which optimize for efficiency (as an expression of win/lose metrics) and not for resiliency and life.

2. The second generator function is **the deconstruction of intrinsic value** itself. The deconstruction of value is the sense that human value does not participate in the intrinsic value of the Real, for the Real is dogmatically declared to have no intrinsic value. Thus, there is no shared identity between the interior of the human being and Reality. There is no common participation in a field of shared intrinsic value. Instead of being intimate with value, we are alienated from value. And only intrinsic value can arouse will: political, moral, and social will.

To sum up, without a shared grammar of value there is no global intimacy, and therefore no global coherence, and no global coordination in response to catastrophic and existential risk, which means, put simply, there will be, quite literally, no future.

HEALING THE GLOBAL INTIMACY DISORDER REQUIRES THE EVOLUTION OF INTIMACY

But we are not hopeless. On the contrary, we are filled with great hope. Hope is a memory of the future. That memory of the future *is* the direct hit that takes down the Death Star, the culture of death. **The direct hit must be**—as it has always been in history—**the emergence of a new stage of evolution**.

Crisis is an evolutionary driver, and every crisis is, at its core, a crisis of intimacy: from the oxygen crisis of the single cells dying which generated multicellular life at the dawn of existence, to the existential risk in this very moment.[9]

The direct hit is therefore structurally self-evident: the evolution of intimacy itself.

What is intimacy, as a structure of Cosmos all the way down and all the way up the evolutionary chain? We engage this inquiry in depth in other writings, but for now we will simply adduce what we have called the "Intimacy Equation":

> *Intimacy = shared identity in the context of [relative] otherness x mutuality of recognition x mutuality of pathos x mutuality of value x mutuality of purpose*

Intimacy is about the capacity of parts to generate a *shared identity* while retaining their otherness, or distinct identity. This requires multiple mutualities, including recognition, pathos (or feeling), value, and purpose. The parts must recognize and feel each other, even as they share value and purpose. But all of this must lead to intimate union—and not pathological

---

9 We demonstrate this principle in some depth in the multi-volume series, *The Universe: A Love Story* (forthcoming) (https://worldphilosophyandreligion.org/early-ontologies), *The Intimate Universe: Global Intimacy Disorder as Cause for Global Action Paralysis* (forthcoming), and in other writings of CosmoErotic Humanism.

fusion, where the distinct identity of the parts disappears—like subatomic particles that successfully become an atom, or two people who successfully become a couple.

THE DECONSTRUCTION OF VALUE IS THE DECONSTRUCTION OF INTIMACY

We have identified the global intimacy disorder as the root cause of existential risk. But the underlying ultimate failure of intimacy is the deconstruction of value itself.

The deconstruction of value means that human value does not participate in any sense of intrinsic value of the Real. This is not about individual *values,* but about *the Field of Value* that underlies all of them. **When the human being**—moved, often sincerely or even nobly, by myriad cultural, historical, and psychological confusions—**claims to have stepped out of the Field of Value, then intimacy itself is deconstructed.**

The deconstruction of value is the deconstruction of intimacy.

In the absence of a shared Story of Value, a story that is an authentic expression of Reality's Eros, a story rooted in *pseudo-Eros* takes center stage and becomes the generator function for existential risk. Our modern pseudo-Eros story is *rivalrous conflict governed by win/lose metrics.* Such a story catalyzes in its wake the second generator function of existential risk: *complicated fragile systems with no allurement or intimacy between the parts.* It is in that sense that we have argued that the first generator function for existential risk is the success story.

- The failure of intimacy is precisely the impotent experience that there is no shared identity between the interior of the human being and Reality. **There is no shared identity in the sense of any kind of common participation in a field of shared intrinsic value.**
- **But only a shared Story of Value can arouse the global will**

required to engage catastrophic and existential risk. For it is only global political, moral, and social will—and we can even say *erotic* will—that can generate the most Good, True and Beautiful world that we have always known is possible.

THE EVOLUTION OF LOVE IS THE TELLING OF A NEW STORY

Coupled with the Intimacy Equation is the scientifically grounded realization, in both the exterior and interior sciences, that Reality is a progressive deepening of intimacies, or, said slightly differently:

Reality is Evolution. Evolution is the evolution of intimacy.

- ◆ The evolution of intimacy requires—both personally and collectively—a deeper, more accurate discernment of the nature of our universe, ourselves, and our Beloveds.
- ◆ This new discernment generates a new global Story of Value.
- ◆ The new global Story of Value generates an emergent, heretofore unseen global intimacy and heals the global intimacy disorder.

The new Story of Value is the direct hit that takes down the Death Star and replaces it with the hope that invokes the memory of our best future.

Global intimacy facilitates global coherence, which facilitates global coordination, which activates the possibility of our creative and effectively coordinated global responses to the global meta-crisis in its entirety and its specific expressions.

To solve Bertrand Russell's challenge—the apparent argument for the subjectivity of ethical values—**we have to reground value theory in eternal yet evolving First Principles and First Values, and articulate a new Story of Value**.

This is what we call CosmoErotic Humanism.

CosmoErotic Humanism—together with other emergent strands—**needs to become the ground of a world religion as a context for our diversity**. We need religion, even as we need science, to articulate a shared global grammar of value.

As we said at the beginning, our choice is simple: love or die.

- To love means to participate in the evolution of love, which is the evolution of the human Story of Value.
- To love means to evolve and activate a new cultural enlightenment—rooted in a new narrative of identity, a new narrative of value, a new narrative of intimate communion, a new narrative of desire, a new narrative of power—all of which will birth new narratives of economics and politics.
- The evolution of love is the telling of a new Story.

The new Story that must be told is a love story, for in fact that is the deepest truth of Reality, rooted in the best exterior and interior sciences, that we have at this moment in time:

- Reality is not merely a fact. Reality is a story.
- Reality is not an ordinary story. Reality is a love story.
- Reality is not an ordinary love story. Reality is an Outrageous Love Story.

Story doesn't mean it's *made-up*.

It means doing the hard work of integrating the validated insights of the traditional world, the modern world, and the postmodern world.

This is the intention at the heart of telling the new Story of CosmoErotic Humanism.

ABOUT THIS VOLUME

Humanity is faced with catastrophic and existential risk. Environmental crisis, technological crisis, political crisis—all are evident and unfolding exponentially at an unprecedented pace.

The vectors of crisis evoke a range of responses:

- Some people respond by looking away—the *denial* response.
- Some respond by falling into despair—the *doomer* response.
- Some respond with bold action to control Reality in order to meet one crisis or another—the *domination* response.

This book responds to existential risk in a fourth way—the da Vinci response, which capacitates our telling of a new Story of Value.[1] It is only from within the context of this new story that we can address the more fundamental disorder that underlies each and every crisis: the global intimacy disorder.

In this book, we present a new story of humanity, a new understanding of our intimate relationship to evolution, as well as our intimacies with ourselves and with our circle of beloveds.

In these pages, we will contemplate the emergence of a new species of humanity, *Homo amor* (previously called *Homo amor universalis)*. You will see that not only are we at a moment of crisis, but we are also present at a moment of birth— the birth of a new humanity. Our crisis is a birth.

---

1   See David J. Temple, *First Principles and First Values: Forty-two Propositions on CosmoErotic Humanism* (2024).

Moreover, you will see that you are personally called to become the new human—because you are an irreducibly unique incarnation of the evolutionary impulse that drives all of Reality. This realization transforms how you relate to yourself and to others, and how you relate to God.

In these pages, you will find meditations and reflections that guide you to identify—if you are willing—the Outrageous Acts of Love, the unique actions that are yours and yours alone to undertake.

In this book, you will hear evolution described in terms that deeply implicate you in the arc of Reality. We are all personally implicated in evolution. And *She* demands from us our irreducibly profound, potent, and powerful partnership. *She* is the ultimate currency of connection, even as *She* is the context for our conversation.

These oral essays are both universal and deeply personal to you, because you are every human. And every human being—under the gaze of love—is a unique expression of the evolutionary impulse that has shaped Reality since the Big Bang.

Volume 8

These oral essays are edited talks delivered by Marc Gafni and Barbara Marx Hubbard between February and April 2018.

CHAPTER ONE

EXPERIENCING EROS THROUGH EVOLVING NEED AND FREEDOM

Episode 71 — February 24, 2018

MEDITATION TO FEEL HOMO AMOR UNIVERSALIS

Take a moment to settle into the present, and bring into your consciousness yourself as a member of the new species *Homo amor universalis*. Experience yourself as part of a new field of consciousness—a field of creativity, a field of innovations, a field of technological genius—woven together into a new whole planetary system that never existed before on this planet.

Now bring your *Unique Self* into the field of *Homo amor universalis* and **feel the wholeness of your being.** All your parts—your spiritual part, your psychological genius, your unique social function—are becoming whole like a cell in the living body that is planet Earth.

Experience your own identity shifting, expanding, to be a whole being within a whole planetary system with all the powers activated. As we move from *Homo Deus* as a being separated from all of this to *Homo amor universalis* as our new species, let us realize that as each of us becomes a conscious member of *Homo amor universalis*, we inform the entire system with our beauty and our contribution, and that simultaneously

1

the whole system informs us that we are part of a new creation. To feel this in every cell of your body, experience your cells waking up to a new day, to a new life, to a new love, *because your cells are sensitive to your consciousness*! Hold that beautiful awareness of who we are as part of this whole.

PRAYER TO THE GOD THAT NEEDS ME

We are going to deepen this understanding of *Homo amor universalis*. What does it mean to answer the great question of who are you? It means:

- I am a member and an expression of this new species.
- I am a unique configuration of the LoveIntelligence and LoveBeauty that initiated and animates All-That-Is.
- I am that which has never expressed itself, ever in history, anywhere other than through me in this unique configuration of love, of *amor*, of *Homo amor universalis*.
- I stand at the edge of the abyss of darkness and I can say, *Let there be light*, and through my unique singularity of light, I can experience *Reality needing me*.

This means that Reality needs my service. As *Homo amor universalis*, we are doing it not just for ourselves. At the Evolutionary Church, we know that we come together to love each other madly, not just for ourselves, but to participate in the evolution of love.

As unique configurations of LoveIntelligence, we are unique configurations of a quality of intimacy which is divinity. In Evolutionary Church we are evolving what it means to be intimate with the Divine; we are evolving prayer and we are evolving God. Conventionally, God has become the Santa Claus god in the sky who manipulates the world: a cosmic vending machine. That's not the god we are talking about. The god you don't believe in doesn't exist.

God is not only the Infinity of Power, who lives also through me, in me, and as me. God is also the Infinity of Intimacy, and so we turn to the Divine who is the Infinity of Intimacy, and we imagine our most intimate moment with a Beloved, with a friend, with a daughter, a son, a mother, a father, an intimate. Imagine your most tender, erotic, gorgeous, pulsing intimate moment, and then exponentialize that moment billions and billions and even more fold, and you can begin to grasp for a moment a flash of awakening.

God is the Infinity of Intimacy who knows our name, who lives in us, as us, and through us, even as She holds us. When Rumi talks about falling into the arms of the Beloved, the Beloved is not just me. The Beloved is *that which holds me*: the Infinity of Intimacy that knows my name and delights in me. I bring all of myself to that altar. I bring my pain, I bring my frustration, I bring my joy, I bring my brokenness, and I bring my *holy and my broken Hallelujah.*

When we evoke Leonard Cohen's holy and broken *Hallelujah*, we evoke all of our lives, all of our stories, and all of our sacred autobiographies:

My sacred autobiography is a chapter in the Divine story.

I am personally implicated in God.

My story is a chapter of the Divine story.

My love story is a chapter of God's love story.

My holy and my broken *Hallelujahs* are all the hidden moments, all the painful moments, all the heartbreaks, and all the breakthroughs—*it all matters.*

We bring it to the altar, we bring the holy and the broken *Hallelujah* to the Beloved. When we pray, we turn to the Divine in that great invitation of one of the great masters, the Baal Shem Tov, who invites us to ask for everything. Not just for world peace, but for everything, because *prayer affirms the dignity of personal need.* We impress our lips on the lips of the

Divine, the Infinity of Intimacy, and we ask for everything. *Hallelujah* in the original Hebrew means *drunken intoxication*. When I am completely down and desperate, *Hallelujah* means *pristine praise* at the same time. What we understand in *Hallelujah* is that every breath I draw, the whole thing is *Hallelujah*.

THE EVOLUTION OF FREEDOM THROUGH THE PLEASURE IMPULSE

Let's dwell for a moment on the meaning of a CosmoErotic personal, psychological, and social, love affair. We have all heard about love affairs of every single possible kind, but I don't think we have ever fully experienced a CosmoErotic personal, psychological, social love affair, on planet Earth.

As a member of this living planetary organism, each person can give their unique gift by joining genius in such a way that it creates a new social body. This social body is the evolution of democracy, the evolution of win/lose, the evolution of separate religions, and separate parties, toward the unique expression of each of us as members of a whole system.

Contemplate that shift from an entire phase of evolution, where *Homo sapiens* has created the most extraordinary genius and a culture with capacities once attributed to ancient gods. **At this phase shift, we are one iota of an evolutionary second from either destroying our whole system with all this power or connecting ourselves to a new system altogether**. We connect ourselves to a new system not by redoing our political structure, nor by recreating our religions, but actually by joining together to give our gift in love to one another on an individual, social, and eventually, planetary scale.

Remember, we are evolution.

We are the impulse of evolution, uniquely as who we are, and that unique impulse in every phase of evolution has increased consciousness from a single-cell to multi-celled organism, to animal, to humans, to *Homo amor universalis*. We are now evoking that consciousness of *Homo amor universalis* by retracing the trajectory of *freedom* from the single-celled organisms, all the way up through individuality, to democracy, to the liberation of sexuality, and now to what? What would freedom mean for *Homo amor universalis* as a CosmoErotic, psycho-social love affair? Get in touch with the extent of your freedom, and consider what it would be like at the next stage of freedom.

Take a moment to check in on that, personally. How does it feel as your consciousness is expanding to include what Sri Aurobindo called *supramental genius*? This is the genius of evolution, liberating you into greater freedom to be fully your potential self as a member of this living system. **Each member of the system gains the power of the whole, just as every cell in your body, whether it be an eye cell, an ear cell, or a liver cell, is gaining the power of being a member of your physical body of trillions of cells.** Each of us is a part of a planetary body. Just imagine the enormous creativity of the planetary body made up of each of us, comparable to the physical body made up of all these individual cells.

So, we are in the planetary body, made up of individual human expressions in greater expanded consciousness, in greater expanded freedom to fulfill Divine potential as part of the larger living system. **Nobody can fulfill our potential for freedom without being part of the greater whole**. The whole John Wayne phase of freedom—*I'm the cowboy, I'm free to do what I want all on my own*—has passed. We can feel right now the freedom to be our full potential selves in the living planetary body in which I am connected in a complex, synergistic coordination of order and love. I am feeling this freedom. Feel it with me! Feel the freedom in your planetary consciousness that is expressing love and joining genius.

Do you see our little planet glowing in the dark? Do you see us, possibly, sending out signals to other life forms as we do this? Do you feel the

CosmoErotic, psycho-social, love affair? And now let's go to the climax here, the evolutionary climax. Nobody talks about what that might be, except us, when we talk about a **Unique Self Symphony**. We talk about a planetary coming-together in love through a Unique Self Symphony. Do you know what that is?

The Unique Self Symphony is a CosmoErotic, ecstatic, organic, coming together.

Could it be that God put all this pleasure into the system to get us to do all this? Just as God put sex in the system to get us to have so many babies because it was very pleasurable. Otherwise, we would never have had that many babies.

It is hard work to get a planet to work with everybody having to get up in the morning and do something challenging. But what if God put the same organic, orgasmic incentive into coming together as a planetary body that God put into reproducing the species? What if God is putting this incentive toward co-evolving through us?

Let's for the moment now, have a flash of genius and imagine the coming together of our social body, where each of our parts gets to be more than it is, because it is part of the organ that it is meant to be part of, just as the imaginal cells in the body of the butterfly are suddenly in awe of what they've created. We, humans, are all doing our separate parts. Let's put ourselves now in the Wheel of Co-Creation, put ourselves in the heart of the hub of the Wheel, with the impulse of creation going through us as our unique identity.

Place yourself where you fit best with the people with whom you love to create. Out of this process, we resolve the separations and conflicts that can't be resolved in the state of consciousness in which they were created. The current win/lose structure of democracy is preventing us from coming together in this way. The structure of various religions prevents us from coming together like this, too.

We are creating a context, an organic whole system context: a CosmoErotic, psycho-social body called *Homo amor* universalis for the very first time expressed through an Evolutionary Church, just as the Catholic Church once spoke of the *second coming of Christ* and changed the world. Let us now call for the first coming of humanity as a whole system, imbued with the impulse of Evolutionary Love transcending all separation and experiencing this together as *Homo amor universalis.*

The pleasure of Eros drives evolution forward.

It is a moment to celebrate. We have let the evangelists—with all blessings to our Evangelical friends—get excited, and we are supposed to be like the Episcopalians—we don't get excited. Let's get excited! Evolutionary Church is reaching thousands of people around the globe! We are in Bethlehem. We're in Kashmir. We're in Beirut. We're in Jerusalem.

For the first time, we are gathering and celebrating this reality, this realization that we live in a CosmoErotic Universe. We are celebrating the realization that Reality is Eros, all the way up and down the evolutionary spiral.

Eros means the experience of radical aliveness, moving toward ever-deeper levels of contact and ever-greater wholes. Now if you think that sentence is easy, it took us about 20 years—it is a big sentence. Just as quarks came together and became atoms, and atoms came together and became molecules, all the way up and all the way down the evolutionary spiral, we live in a CosmoErotic Universe. Eros is the movement and experience of radical aliveness, living in me, moving toward ever-greater contact and ever larger wholes.

That experience of moving toward greater wholeness is pleasurable. That is pleasure. Consider a term from Kashmir Shaivism that echoes this reality—*Sat Chit Ananda*:

- *Sat* is being,
- *Chit* is consciousness,
- *Ananda* is bliss, or love,

So, the inside of being is consciousness, and the inside of consciousness is bliss or love.

The Inside of the Inside is pleasure, *Ananda*, pleasure, bliss, love.

The interiority of eternity is pleasure. But the interiority of *evolution* is pleasure. Evolution IS Eros, and evolution is the movement toward more contact and greater wholes. Evolution manifested and birthed this great *evolution of love* which is the realization that evolution is conscious. Now we realize that this Conscious Evolution is driven by Evolutionary Love and Evolutionary Love is manifesting, literally, in this church as we join genius and name the new species.

We have talked about *Homo Deus*, which is a book by a colleague of ours, Yuval Harari. While we love and respect you, Yuval, in your cynical view of the desiccated, merely random, non-intimate world in which people are striving for immortality to cover over their gaping emptiness, we think you missed it.

Actually, we are *Homo amor universalis.*

UNIQUE SELF AND THE EVOLUTION OF NEED

What does that mean? The individual of *Homo amor* universalis is what we call the Evolutionary Unique Self. What is a Unique Self? Let's look at it through the lens of need. Every one of us has a set of six core human needs. Every one of us, no exception.

We have this need to be intended. Imagine your Beloved thinks about your anniversary on the day of your anniversary and then says, *It is our anniversary! I forgot, let me get you flowers.* That doesn't feel good. You want your Beloved to think about it a couple of weeks before.

Here are the six core needs:

- We have to know we're *intended*,
- We want to know we're *chosen*, to be the chosen one.
- We want to know that we're *recognized*.
- We want to know that we're *adored*.
- We want to know that we're *desired*.
- We want to know that we're *needed*.

These six core human needs are important. If you want to put together the best, deepest, inner psychological, spiritual, existential, emotional, and psychoanalytical understanding, it is that we have six core human needs. Every human being needs to be intended. We need to be chosen, we need to be recognized, we need to be adored, we need to be desired, and we need to be needed.

Now look what we do: **we tend to take those needs and then we find one person in the world and we say we want you to meet all those needs**. I need you to recognize me, I need you to adore me, I need you to intend me, I need you to love me, and I need you to need me, and I need you to choose me, and if for one second that one person to whom we've exiled all these needs fails to meet them, we're devastated. We want to get them all met by that one person.

When we are not desired by that one person at that one moment, we are broken, we are depressed, and we take opioids. You know why? **We are devastated because we are alienated from the core structure of Reality**. I cannot get those six core human needs met by one person. One person can't incarnate them. I can have one person, or a circle of people—sons, daughters, friends, intimate lovers, wives, husbands—fulfill a dimension of those needs.

But all those human beings who are fulfilling those needs are reflections of Source. Imagine there is a rock shining on the ocean. You are on the ocean, you are on the beach and you see this rock shining. You just completely fixate on the shining rock, but then the sun moves, the rock disappears, and you are devastated. It's not the rock, it's the sun.

To be an Evolutionary Unique Self—a Unique Self living in evolutionary context, awake and aware of Conscious Evolution—is to know *that* **Reality** *intended me*. **Reality intended me, Reality intended each of us, and Reality intended all of us. Way before I came, Reality intended me.**

Then Reality chose us and Reality desired us. It is kind of shocking that Reality desires Barbara, Reality desires Marc, Reality desires each of us. I'm desired by Reality itself and Reality needs my service, Reality adores me.

When I begin to experience that's the nature of who I am, I begin to awaken beyond rivalrous conflict.

When I know that I am adored, I'm desired, I'm needed, I'm recognized, I'm intended, I'm chosen, I awaken beyond the need to poach on someone else's space, beyond the need to be constantly grasping. I begin to awaken as *Homo amor* universalis and we begin to come together in intimacy.

AUTONOMY AND COMMUNION ARE RESOLVED IN INTIMACY

Let's go to the Inside of the Inside. The biggest conflict in the world is, *I want to be autonomous*, (me, independent, John Wayne) and, *I want to be in communion* (I want to be close, intimate). Whole philosophical traditions said the only real thing is autonomy. Like America, in any community we have, it is a social contract: *We give up some rights to the government to create community, but only the individual is real*. Communism said the opposite: *No, only the state is real, only the community is real, and the individual exists only to serve the state*. This huge conflict has never been solved, and we can't create a new world of wholeness, we can't create new cities—which we will desperately need to do as refugees mount—we can't create new societies unless we can resolve that conflict.

Homo amor universalis resolves that conflict because *Homo amor universalis* is an Outrageous Lover. We live in a world of outrageous pain and only the response is Outrageous Love. **Autonomy and communion are resolved in ecstasy**: I'm ecstatic, awake, and alive, filled with Eros.

Then I want to be in devotion to you. My freedom, my autonomy, my delight is to be in devotion. Typically, we are afraid to be in devotion; we have lost the quality of devotion. But in **Unique Self Symphony we are devoted to each other, and there is no clash between autonomy and communion because we are each irreducibly unique**. Marc can't be Barbara, or anyone else, as that's never going to happen. So, I get to meet my friend Swamiji and be in radical delight and devotion. I'm ecstatic that Reality manifested Swamiji. We get to meet each other and be madly in love with each other. We get to be mad lovers.

Autonomy and communion are resolved in ecstasy, and here's the last step: **autonomy and communion are resolved in intimacy**. *Homo amor universalis* knows we live in an Intimate Universe. Intimacy means shared identity: it's not just *me*, it's *we*. But *we* is not a technical function, and it's not a survival game. We actually share our identity.

We have talked about the evolutionary impulse, the evolutionary imperative. This evolutionary impulse is what pounds in me, throbs in me, and is awake and alive in me. Its first expression is sexuality, its second expression is innovation, but its deepest expression is transformation. **The deepest transformation, and the greatest pleasure, is the transformation of identity**.

Are we willing to participate now in the Evolution of Love? Are we willing to play a larger game and transform our identity? Not for ourselves, but to evolve love, to bring down *Homo amor* universalis? Friends, this is all personal, I am personally implicated in this story. This is not philosophy or theoretical. This is *I am Homo amor universalis*. **To love is to know that I am a unique configuration of intimacy, a unique expression of** the LoveIntelligence, and that I can stand at the edge of the abyss of darkness and say, *Let there be light* with my love.

As *Homo amor universalis*, I love the moment open.

CHAPTER TWO

OUR PERSONAL LOVE STORIES ARE PART OF A PLANETARY BIRTH STORY

Episode 72 — March 3, 2018

A MEDITATION ON MASS ALLUREMENT

Consider a vision of a world of mass allurement, mass resonance, where each one of us is resonating individually with the whole system. If we go the whole way beyond our Earth, we'd say it is the cosmic system of which planet Earth is a member and of which we are all members. From the perspective of the individual, place yourself now in your deepest empathetic feeling of wholeness and oneness with your family, and now, with this church. **This is the very first church to hold the field of the love story of the universe, within a cosmos that is all connected.**

Place yourself in your particular function in the social body where you are called to be your Unique Self. Feel yourself like a cell in the planetary body uniquely called as one part of a social system. Feel the organ that you're part of in the social body coming together to create new forms of health, new forms of education, new forms of media. See yourself resonating as a member of that body through your unique expression of who you are.

Now feel the planetary body going through a crisis of separation, dislocation, and possible danger. See it as the crisis of the birth of this planetary organism, coming together with the difficulty of all births. Think of the difficulty of having a baby. Now, let's just for this moment think about how we feel when we first see the newborn, whether we are a mother or a father, a sister, or a brother. But for the moment just be a mother who has gone through the labor and pain of birth. Out comes this amazing organism and we're holding that baby in our arms. **We are right this moment holding this baby calling for the cosmic awakening of humanity.** Let's go the whole way and imagine the cosmos being part of this process that we are in, to awaken us at the deepest levels of our being.

THE GOD WITHIN US AND THE GOD HOLDING US

The revolution in evolution is happening here. This is the vision of the future. Consider that the Civil Rights Movement in the United States happened based on the Gospel Church. Without the Gospel Church, my friends, there was no Civil Rights Movement.

The Gospel Church meant that:

- We came together in community and we loved each other madly.
- We came together in the outrageous pain and we found each other in Outrageous Love.
- We came together in the holy and the broken *Hallelujahs* of life and we found each other held in the arms of the Divine.

From this place, we look at our code today:

Allurement guides your life.

We come together in Evolutionary Church, and we are the Gospel Church— we're excited, and we're singing, and we're delighted and we're held in the arms of God. When we say we're held in the arms of God, we always have a simple principle. The principle is that *the god you don't believe in doesn't exist.* It's not the Santa Claus god who lives someplace in the sky and has nothing to do with us, demands our obedience, is slightly sadistic, and outlaws most forms of pleasurable activity that we want to enjoy. It's not that god. It's not the god who says only the Christians are good and not the Jews, or who says only the Jews are good, or only the Tibetan Buddhists are good, or only the Croatians are good and not the Serbs, and only the Hutus are good and not the Tutsis. Meaning, it is not the ethnocentric god, owned by one people. It's not the cosmic vending-machine god where you put in a quarter and get out a red car. It's not the law-of-attraction god, where I use the law of attraction to get my red car. No, it's not *that* god.

It is the God who is, on the one hand, the incessant, ceaseless, creativity of the cosmos that pulses in every second, the self-organizing principle moving Reality in Eros to ever larger wholes and ever-deeper contact— greater love. And on the other hand it is **the God who is beyond the cosmos, who births the cosmos, and who holds us in every moment.** It is the God in whose arms we fall, the God about whom we know in our bodies—in our hearts, and our guts, and our toenails—that *every place I fall, I fall into Her hands.* And knowing that on the one hand, she lives in me, as me, and through me—She's the evolutionary impulse awakening as me—and on the other hand, She is beyond me and She holds me, tenderly caressing me, knowing everything about my life and being more interested in every detail of my life than the closest girlfriend or boyfriend could imagine to be. God is loving me madly, desiring me, holding me tenderly, quivering, delighting in my life and wanting my good.

Every place I fall, I fall into Her hands—that is the God we are talking about.

The first face of God, the God that pulses through Reality and births Reality, is power, exponentialized into infinity. That's the God who's the Infinity of Power—feel this new field of language we're laying down together as the Gospel Church did. Feel it, as we sing our way, as we love our way, to the *democratization of enlightenment*. And the second face of God is not merely the Infinity of Power, but what we call here in Evolutionary Church, in a key meme, God who is the Infinity of Intimacy.

Imagine, sometimes when we are working hard, and we say, let's have a little intimacy now, we mean relax into the intimate space of just *being* together. Imagine that space where there is no place to go, and there is nothing to do, and there's nothing that needs to be said, but you are resting in goodness. Sometimes we have that when we are eating lunch. We are eating the most fabulous food in the world. There is an intimacy between us and the food, and at just that moment when we are biting and the succulent tastes pour through our body, we say *ahhh, Reality is self-evidently good*. In intimacy, we are already here, there's no place to go.

In intimacy, we know that every breath we draw is *Hallelujah*. And *Hallelujah* is the good news. We are founding together—in Bethlehem and in Alabama, and in Athens with Socrates, and in the Far East in Asia, and in every city in the world—an Evolutionary Church with the gospel, the good news, and the good news is the new story. It is the new story of power, and it's the new story of intimacy, in which we are personally implicated. And we realize in church, God/Goddess, She is the Infinity of Intimacy, and it is good right now, and it is good to be together, right now. From that place of beingness and goodness, in which we know as we say *Hallelujah!* *Hallelujah* means in Hebrew *hallel*, pristine praise, the outrageous beauty, and *holelut,* the drunken intoxication of the outrageous pain. But it is all held, and from that place of knowing, it is all held and no one is extra, and nothing is extra. From that place, we're going to build a new world and from that place, we are inspired.

A TECHNICOLOR VISION OF THE PLANETARY BIRTH

When I (Barbara) was in the Notre Dame Cathedral and saw how they celebrated, most extraordinarily, the birth and the resurrection of Christ, it made me think. I asked myself *What can we do as great as what they did when they celebrated the birth of Christ through those massive, magnificent cathedrals?*' Here is what I received in response: a vision, just like a Technicolor movie.

Join me as I share this vision, which is our Universe Story—but this is a particular version of it about birth.

Feel the Earth as a living organism, heaving for breath, struggling to coordinate as one body. Let us just feel the Earth as a living system. It is alive, the whole thing. Now, become a cell in that body. You are that, I am that, we are that, and the prayers that everyone is offering are our prayer from the body of Earth, in the body of the universe. We are going from micro to macro here. **The pain of this whole planetary body has been flashing through our mass media—the hunger, the disease, the refugees, and the wars—all of this has been flashing through our nervous system.** We have been feeling children starving, soldiers dying, mothers crying, and people burning alive. The agony of our Earth is ours.

Every one of us is a member of this planetary body feeling this pain right now: her polluted waters, her clogged air, her depleted soil, the destruction of her forest. It is all happening to us. She and we are one. **There is no other, there is no outside, we are one living body, all of us.** Now, let us speed up the movie. We are watching a technicolor movie. We have been feeling mainly through our media, and through our knowledge of what's happening.

Now, see a flash of extraordinary light more radiant than the sun gleaming in outer space. If you can imagine how that sun looks when you can see it gleaming, this light is more radiant than that. For the moment, forget all our pain. We stop crying and we see this light, together. It catches our attention for one brief instant. With that moment of shared attention, let's imagine ourselves as members of one planetary body that has been feeling so much pain and so much stress, individually, and as a whole, and suddenly stopped to share a moment of attention in which we see something as radiant as a cosmic sun. **Empathy is beginning to course through our bodies.** All our prayers that we've been offering together are being answered.

Yes, all of our prayers. Planet Earth is a big house and we are all connected. There is no outside, this is exactly right. A magnetic Field of Love is aligning us. This is a cosmic Technicolor movie and it is also happening right here. We are caressed and uplifted by that light. Feel it. **If we say we are one living body, let's feel being one body with that light of Source.** Joy is beginning to pulse through our bodies and through the allurements of being connected to one another. If allurement is our life, then one by one, imagine the allurement when we feel ourselves to be members of a whole body in deep connection with each other.

A magnetic field of light. We are caressed in this field of light. Joy is infusing through our bodies. Just think for a moment of that little first smile on the face of a newborn after the struggle and pain of birth. Just think of that little smile. We feel light rising from within, and miracles and healings are occurring. Think of what happened when Jesus walked through a village. He just walked, the blind see, the lame are walking, the deaf are hearing, people are flooding out of their houses to see what's happening. Jesus is a perfect example because when he walked through a village they just came out of their houses. They felt such intensity of Christ's love, that they were healed. That's what we are saying now, that is us. That's exactly how we're feeling.

The Christ energy is within all of us, as us.

We're flooding out of our houses. We are singing together in spontaneous harmonies, a planetary choir of voices, all singing out loud for the first time. This is our first Technicolor movie. Think of the choir singing in those beautiful cathedrals. We are going to do this. This is going to be seen by the world. We sing together in spontaneous harmonies, a planetary choir of voices, all singing out loud a chanting rhythm, beating through the earth, synchronizing our heartbeats. *Boom, boom, boom.* Now let's hear the music come on, while we are seeing the light and the allurement is connecting us.

No division of race, color, nation, or class can hold against the process and the attraction of allurement.

Think of The Universe: A Love Story. Quark to quark, particle to particle, Reality is attraction and allurement, all the way up and all the way down. Now, we are feeling it intensified because it's a moment of collective opening: our thoughts are connected, and we experience the awesome intelligence of ourselves as one planetary living body. Everything that anybody needs to know about, anything is known somewhere in this system, and now, we know it all. The weapons are melting, the air is clearing, the waters are purified, the land is being renewed. We can breathe again. We've gone through the birth canal. It's why it's so frightening to the newborn because the newborn can't breathe in the birth canal.

The pain of the earth is dissolving the mass media. Our nervous system is now pulsing with light. It carries stories of our transformation: We see our rockets rising majestically through the blue sky of space. We are reaching outward to space as we are coordinating inward in inner space, as one gesture in time. Just as a baby's reach for an object outside its own body helps it coordinate, so our reach into space is speeding up the integration of all our systems. Billions of us are opening our collective eyes for the very first time.

We are smiling our first planetary smile. We are members of that whole planetary body. With these words it is like the first smile of a newborn baby when its little nervous system finally links up into coherence. Our little nervous system is just linking up. We are opening our collective eyes. We are seeing our mother and smiling that amazing, radiant smile. How does the baby know its mother? Consider if you are a mother, how did your baby recognize you? Well, how do we recognize our Mother/Father God? The creator of all of us, that is why we recognize it.

As that baby knows her mother, so we, humankind, know the Light.

The light is our Mother/Father. Even though we've never seen it together, each of us in a secret place in our hearts, has experienced the light. Let's just feel it now: the inner light that does not come from us personally, it comes from the entire evolutionary story of creation. It is not only a trajectory from the Big Bang to us, but *is us* at a moment of collective awareness of the whole system that has never before been experienced on Earth. It wasn't yet time.

Ecstatic joy is rippling through the planetary body. We shout to ourselves: *We are being born. Our story is a birth, I know it because it's happening to me right now. I feel overwhelming gratitude.* We have tumbled through this complete, awesome, evolutionary story of creation through allurement and attraction. Now here we are, the first generation capable of planetary birth. The first generation capable of being connected as a whole and capable of feeling the allurements, not only particle to particle, and cell to cell, but the planetary body as a whole being allured unto itself.

Connected with the awesome power of the creation of the universe itself. We are lighting up in the universe as a planet being born in the universe, undoubtedly, filled with life. Let's send the signal to each other. **This is the church of the planetary birth of humanity as one living body, born into a universe of infinite intelligence and life and with this.**

MY PERSONAL LOVE STORY IS IMPLICATED IN THE UNIVERSE: A LOVE STORY

Now that we've seen the macro-vision of planetary birth, let's take a look at the other side, which is the intimate detail of the birth story. We have to hold both sides together and really feel it. Our code is: *Allurement guides my life.* I am a Unique Self, and to be a Unique Self is to have a unique set of allurements. My birth is part of the great birth story.

We have to always be in the integrity of our light, which is the integrity of the awareness of who we are and what needs to be done—what is required, what is demanded, what is invited, and what is allured. I need to always be in the practice of moving between the largest frame and the most intimate frame.

The largest frame of allurement is that *Reality, the universe is a love story.* I (Marc) remember about four or five years ago, I was sitting in New York, sitting and watching children play outside, and I was writing. All of a sudden, literally through my hand the sentence I was writing changed. I saw these sentences written in front of me that had nothing to do with me. The sentences said,

- Reality is not a fact, it's a story.
- It's not an ordinary story, it's a love story.
- It's not an ordinary love story, it's an Outrageous Love Story.
- It's an Evolutionary love story.
- The Universe: A Love Story.

I looked at what was written in front of me, and I hadn't written it. That's allurement. That is a moment where She speaks through us. From that moment on, I realized that those few sentences that She had downloaded through this pen that I happened to be holding (although it wasn't a pen, it was a keyboard) were the organizing principle of my life, of your life, of Barbara's life, and of Reality itself: The Universe: A Love Story.

The universe didn't become a love story today; the universe has always been a love story. The universe was a love story from the first moment of its inception, but the next great momentous leap is *when we understand* that the universe is a love story. That is when the plot changes.

In the old plot of The Universe: A Love Story, God was the lover. We were somehow insignificant and we were deemed worthy of grace because God loved us. In The Universe: A Love Story, there was one great actor—that was God. That was the plot line of The Universe: A Love Story. We now know that **The Universe: A Love Story is not only the Infinity of Intimacy, the infinity of love that holds *us*, but actually, that love story is happening *everywhere*.**

Now, we realize that the love story is happening between three quarks who need to love each other to survive in the first nanosecond of the Big Bang. That love story is happening at every level of molecular, cellular, cosmological, biological, and cultural reality. The whole story is about the exchange between centers of allurement, and each of us is a unique configuration of allurement.

To get the love story is to get out of the pseudo-allurement, get out of the pseudo-desire, and clarify the nature of my allurement.

It is not about the one great prophet who has the experience and we listen to the experience. What we saw in the vision of the planetary birth was that we are all participating in that birth together. I am personally implicated in the great love story of Reality. My love story, which is the story of my allurements, is not about just the one guy or girl, or transgender whom I happen to love.

My love story is every detail. It is what I am allured to when I've *clarified my allurements*. I'm not lost in working things out. I have worked on my early childhood stuff. I've worked out the areas of my life that pull me into the vortex of pain and emptiness. I am aware when they're happening: I can wake up and I can unclench in real-time. Everyone remembers the moment when you were most embarrassed in life, where you were enraged, upset, and clenched, and your highest self was not in play and your lower self ruled the day. That is when you lost touch. We all have had moments like that when we were short, and we were brusque, and we slammed down the phone. That was when we lost our connection to allurement.

How do we regain our connection to allurement? We regain our connection to allurement first by going large and then going small. First, the big screen, is what we laid out in the vision of a planetary birth. A stunning realization that the entire story is what we call here The Universe: A Love Story. There is a birth happening. There's a momentous leap happening in that story, in this moment in time. It's also about realizing that this church is the planetary awakening in love through Unique Self Symphonies. Second, I go small, but not small in a small way; I go *intimate*.

I go into my life and I realize that allurement guides my life. My life is a text of revelation.

This week was the holiday of *Purim*: the holiday of allurement. *Purim* is the one book in the bible in which the name of God is not mentioned. Do you know why the name of God is not mentioned? In Hebrew, the original Hebrew, the name of God is *allurement, is love*. It is a four-letter name, *Yud Hei Vav Hei*—Four letters—and each one of those letters is a story of Eros. The *Yud*, the point enters the *Hei*. The last two letters, the *Vav* and the *Hei* refer to the *Hei* who receives the *Vav*. The *Vav* and the *Hei*, which is the masculine and feminine letters, are allured to each other—they enter each other. So, the name of God is allurement.

So then why in *Purim* is there no name of God in the story? Because *Purim* is the story of public culture and political intrigue. There is no name of God because we realize in our non-dual, total awakening to the true nature of Reality, that you can't speak the name of God as a special name. After all, the name of God is everywhere. **There is no name of God in this political story because this political story, every political story, and every personal story, *is* the name of God.** You specifically designate a name of God only when all the other words are *not* the name of God. This story is one of the 24 books of the biblical canon and is considered to be the highest story. This book is the holiest, this holy day is the holiest of all holy days—*sanctum sanctorum*, Holy of Holies.

God's name is the whole story: the whole story is allurement. My whole life is allurement.

This realization became clear at one of our wisdom schools. We did an exercise: Identify the parts of your life that are a love story. Find the love stories in your life. Every single person in the room as they did this awesome, sacred autobiography writing exercise realized:

> I can't identify the parts of my life that are a love story because my whole life is a love story. The whole thing, my entire life is a tapestry of allurement, and God/Goddess is whispering in my ear and saying come closer, like this, come closer. In the intimate details of my life, in the Infinity of Intimacy which is my life, I realize that my personal life is allurement.

Feel this in your life: *my life is allurement*. The teaching is twofold. First, *my life is allurement*, and second, *allurement guides my life*. Can you feel that? I can get underneath and realize that allurement guides my life. Go to a moment in your life and try and find out how you made every major decision in your life: where to live, who to be with, and who to leave, when to stay, and what to follow.

When you were clear and awake and alive, what guided you?

Why are we here together in this church? Why do we join genius? We're here because allurement guides my life.

Imagine that you are sitting at a restaurant, and you are talking with someone about something in your life. You know, should I move to Acapulco or not? And then you hear someone at the next table and they say, *Wow the real estate is really good in Acapulco*. You say to yourself, *what a coincidence! I can't believe it. I'm thinking about moving to Acapulco and the person at the next table is saying that Acapulco has good real estate.* You think that's a coincidence. No, allurement guides my life. Every place I've been, I needed to be.

The practice of Evolutionary Church is to write your story as the cosmic birth experience. Because it's not one priest, it is a *mamlechet kohanim*, a nation of priests. Write your story and find the little intimate moments in your life where She was speaking directly to you and saying *this is what you need to do. This is your next step. This is the way you need to unfold.* And you begin to realize that She is whispering in your ear every second, She needs you, and your story is personally implicated in the Evolutionary Love Story.

The new plot of the love story is that your love story is somehow, mystically, truly, and essentially central to the love story of all of Reality. You begin to hear the children in Jerusalem dancing in the streets, the dogs barking with joy, and—as we said—the planetary smile emerges on your face. Your face becomes not just a personal smile, but the planetary smile itself. And your joy is not your personal joy, but it is your personal joy as the planetary joy, and your transformation is not just your personal transformation, but the planet itself transforming as you.

Allurement guides my life—not pseudo-allurement, not pseudo-desire, not bypassing. These are all the allurement of the narcissist who does not feel true allurement. Let's find our true universal, connected, allurement, of being One, and our simultaneous uniqueness. Let's find our sameness and our power to synergistically co-create in joy and pleasure which is our deepest desire.

This is going to be a little bit of a hard thing to hear: **to really find your allurement you have to give something up.** You have to give up the clench, the moment of egoic involvement, the moment of self-reference. You have to give up egoic involvement because the way you truly find your allurement is when you are in devotion. You're in devotion to your

Beloved—It might be a Beloved friend, someone you live with, someone you work intimately with, or someone you co-create with—and then you are in devotion not only to your Beloved but to your community, and the entire Evolutionary Church.

Then as an Evolutionary Church we are in devotion, not to Marc and Barbara, but to each other. **All of us in Evolutionary Church are in devotion to the allurement of this planetary love story, a *planetary awakening in love through Unique Self Symphony.***

We are in devotion and we give something up for it. We make a contribution to it and we step into it and we go into the hard place, my friends. If there's no hard place, then you're not looking for allurement, and you are not in the right place. There's always outrageous pain and Outrageous Love and there is always a moment when I have to *bracket myself*. **I have to unclench, I have to clarify my allurement to find that deepest truth**. Then I step into that deepest truth and the planet smiles for me.

Allurement guides my life, and I have to listen to that revelation.

That revelation calls me, and that revelation says, *Come closer, like this. I've been waiting for you. I need you. I desire you. I recognize you. I love you. I see you.* Your allurement says *the divine awakens me, arouses me, makes me whole, and makes me full.* I go to the quietest place, and I listen to my life and I might write my sacred autobiography. Oh my god, we feel: *allurement guides our lives.* We are here because all of us were guided to each other because we're allured. Feel the power of that. Allurement guides our lives.

CHAPTER THREE

THE PRACTICE OF OPENING THE HEART IN THE LOVE STORY OF THE UNIVERSE

Episode 73 — March 10, 2018

FEELING INTO THE RESONANT FIELD OF LOVE

As you are reading this, you are resonating with the impulse of evolution from the billions of years of creativity from single cells to multi-cells to animals to humans to right now in the Evolutionary Church. Everybody's impulse is uniquely their own frequency while resonating with the awesome reality of the whole system.

When your unique frequency goes into a resonant field with two or more, resonating simultaneously with each other's inner impulse of creation, what do we co-create? We create a field, and because the purpose of the Evolutionary Church is to co-create a Field of Universal Evolutionary Love in the world, we are here to create that field as a gift to the world.

Our resonant field has an awesome power, because when we really step into the field, we feel each other—I feel you, feeling me, feeling you—which creates intimacy.

THE FIELD OF INTIMACY: YOUR NEED IS MY ALLUREMENT

Resonance is a resonant field, and in a resonant field it's not only cognitive, although it has a cognitive dimension. But resonance means I feel the field. What is the quality of the field?

The code is:

> Allurement guides my life.
>
> Allurement is resonance. Allurement is the inner feeling, the quality of the field. We speak into the Field of Allurement to draw towards us that which we need so that we can be awake, Outrageous Lovers. We are here as Outrageous Lovers to live in the Field of Allurement. One of the Tenets of Intimacy is: *We live in an Intimate Universe.*

What is intimacy? *Intimacy is shared identity.* It's really simple, four words. **Intimacy is shared identity**. What is the way into shared identity? The way is to *let* myself feel my allurement. How do I feel my allurement? I say, *I feel you.* I'm feeling you, but we're feeling each other:

- ◆ Level 1 is I feel you, and then you feel me.
- ◆ Level 2 is *I feel you feel me.*
- ◆ Level 3 is I feel you feeling me, and you feel me feeling you.

So, if I have a fever, you have a fever. If I'm awake, you're awake. If you're concerned, I'm in anxiety. Not in a codependent, neurotic way, but in the way of Evolutionary Lovers. Then it becomes a triple loop of intimacy: I feel you, feeling me, feeling you.

If you want to understand prayer, prayer is about Source's allurement to us. **Prayer is God in search of man; Goddess in search of woman.** To pray is to create and invoke the new human and the new humanity. To become that new human is to feel into the Field of Allurement and realize that *I'm guided,* but not only by the rational, nor by the superstitious, nor by the

28

dogma. We let go of the dogma. We hold the best of the rational, but we go deeper, and access the super-rational underneath the rational. The rational itself is part of a larger Field of Allurement, which is intimate.

In intimacy, it is not so much about the technical details of who's who. It's not about guarding my space. Yes, we do all that. Yes, we're separate selves, but underneath separate selves, we're intimate together. We have a shared identity.

The tension between autonomy and communion is resolved in intimacy, because in intimacy we have a shared identity.

It is not simply that we are God—God is God and I am me; but also I am God, and God is me.

They're both true. Autonomy and communion don't disappear, but the tension between them is resolved in intimacy.

We're *godding* together even as God holds us. Do you get how deep that is? When we pray, we turn to the Divine and say,

> My Goddess, please, I love you so madly. Would you hold my holy and my broken *Hallelujah*? Would you hold my pain? Would you hold my yearning? Would you hold my tension? Would you please hold my broken heart?

We can feel the Divine say to us, *Your need is my allurement*. We have a shared identity with the Divine. **To live in an intimate universe means to have a shared identity with divinity**, and for divinity to have a shared identity with me, even as She's beyond me, holding me at the same time.

That's why we bring the dignity of our need to prayer, in erotic union with the Infinity of Intimacy which is the Divine. All of it, our holy and our broken *Hallelujah*, everything, every issue: my body, my age, my health, my budget, my need—it's all holy: *your need is my allurement.*

A UNIQUE SELF SYMPHONY DRIVEN BY ALLUREMENT

We pray for the planetary awakening in love. We pray for the experience of the Unique Self Symphony. The Unique Self Symphony is everybody's unique vibrational field symphonizing. It's not just going along adjacent to each other, but creating a resonant field of intimacy. Imagine the Unique Self Symphony moving toward an apex of convergence, just as nature does. It converges that which is arising. That's how we got here. Put yourself now as one of those Unique Self Symphony vibrational fields going up into the apex of an awakening in love at a planetary scale.

If God is love, then let's put into this moment of history that we are in The Universe: A Love Story. That is to say, we are not just now beginning to come together in love; rather, we are the current culmination of 13.7 billion years of joining to create, a culmination accelerated by crisis. Think of the vibrational field that comes out of the Big Bang. Think of those quarks. They were *allured* to each other. It's hard to think of quarks being allured, but they were. Then, think of the protons and the neutrons. Then imagine single cells all by themselves being allured to form multicellular organisms.

> *The degree to which allurement enables the joining of genius at every level is the degree to which allurement has literally created the universe.*

Most of the time when scientists look at the story of evolution, they see evolution by competition. **We are seeing evolution by co-creativity, by joining through love, by joining genius.** A cell has genius. A single DNA joins genius awesomely, all the way on up. Rather than selecting for what competes best, and wins over all the others, it appears that over these billions of years, nature has been selecting for what *cooperates* best. To create all these large-scale organisms, now creating a planetary organism of sorts, where we are facing this exact crisis of systems of separation that are breaking down and, in the very same moment *cooperation, co-creation, joining genius, synergy, and love,* is also arising.

This Church of Evolutionary Love is the first church ever designed to awaken Evolutionary Love at a planetary scale at a time of breakdown. **In this time of breakdown, a breakthrough in Evolutionary Love is precisely what the world needs to evolve.**

The church of Evolutionary Love is a church of universal love by allurement, planetary allurement, and global allurement. In this church, there are many initiatives and projects, and that is good because not any one of them alone is enough, but all of them are arising toward convergence, through allurement and resonance, and are being empowered by the convergence.

I don't think any of the great projects, including the Evolutionary Church, would work all by itself at a global scale, or even at any scale. Let's take a moment now just to feel inside ourselves that our life is guided by allurement; not only our life, but life in general, is guided by allurement and resonance.

One project is synergistic democracy. The current win/lose structure of democracy, which was so powerful in an age of monarchy, today tends to divide; and there is no way we can create a whole global communion with divisions at every stage of the current structure of democracy. **Synergistic democracy is a system of joining genius in every field, in every function, in every country, by allurement**. Is this a good political program? I can imagine so since I (Barbara) arrived at the Democratic National Convention to propose an Office for the Future to map, track, and connect what's working. Let's go even further, to a global political convention, and speak of synergistic democracy that arises globally through allurement.

This would spread on the internet, in a global awakening in the nervous system of humanity, in which this church is the first church to declare as its purpose the awakening of humanity in love, through being love ourselves.

A PLANETARY AWAKENING REQUIRES AN OPEN HEART

What needs to happen to make a planetary awakening in love through Unique Self Symphonies come true? It is only possible when I can open my heart. I have to peel away layers covering my heart. We often think it is happening out there.

We think that there are two tracks in the world. There's my personal love story, the details of my life, the places where I'm stuck, clenched, or contracted, where I am the little boy or the little girl. That's one life. Then there's the big life, the save the world and transform humanity life, and somehow we need to keep those two things as separate as we can from each other so one does not ruin the other. That's how we always think. There's the big stuff we do, then there's the details.

We can invoke a planetary awakening in love through Unique Self Symphony only when I begin to realize that **my love story is connected to a larger set of planetary actions**. I'm speaking of my love story right now as I'm talking, as I'm texting, as I'm loving, as I'm creating, as I'm engaging with my colleagues, my friends, my staff, my world, my boards, my students. Let's say I'm running an organization. How I'm paying my staff and how I'm doing the integrity of my payments, the whole thing is a love story.

It's all a love story, friends. There is nothing that is not a chapter and verse in my love story. And my love story is chapter and verse in The Universe: A Love Story.

To be asleep in the world is when you are in a love affair and you're not aroused—and *arousal*, by the way, is a word we have exiled to this very narrow dimension which is sexuality. Arousal in sexuality is of course beautiful—but arousal in sexuality models the greatest arousal, which is *I'm aroused in life.*

I am *er*. The word *er* in Hebrew means awake and aroused. ER, it is the emergency room. It's *ayin reish*, in Hebrew, *er* means I'm aroused or awake. *Sometimes I'm sleeping*, says Solomon of the Song of Songs, *but my heart is aflame and aroused. Let my heart guide me. Let me have an aroused and aflame heart.*

To be asleep means I'm in the middle of my love affair with Reality in every dimension and Reality is making love to me and I'm lost in my clench. I'm asleep, and I can't find my way out. Do you know how absurd it is? Imagine the paradoxical, grotesque, theater of the absurd: Reality is making love to me and I'm not aroused. The word, *er*, aroused, or awake is the same word in the original Hebrew, *er* spelled backwards, is *ra*, evil. **Evil is the failure of arousal**.

We think arousal leads to all evil, but true arousal means I'm aroused in life. I'm allured to you. Your need is my allurement. We can feel each other.

The way to create a planetary awakening in love through Unique Self Symphony is to begin with the person right next to me.

It does not work by bypassing the people in my circle of intimacy and influence. It means the world becomes a Unique Self Symphony in which every person is in Evolutionary Church right now, and each of us has two people in our circle that we have a clench with, and we unclench that closed place—and then we expand, each one of us expands our circle by one person—one person that has been left out, one person that is out of the circle. So, we unclench with the two people we are clenched with and we invite one person into the circle, and we have a planetary awakening in love through Unique Self Symphony.

That's what the planetary Pentecost is about. When Christ talks about the Pentecost, he is not talking about bypassing. On the other hand, communism, Marxism, and Hegelian thought bypassed the individual to heal the world. These early evolutionary spirituality movements said *let's wake up the world*, but along the way we have to kill 17 million collective farmers in Ukraine. Along the way we have to have Gulag Archipelago where parents betrayed children, and the children betrayed their parents. Along the way we have Big Brother and George Orwell.

No, the way to awaken and be an evolutionary Outrageous Lover is, I find the clench inside of me right now, in that which is closest to me. That's what the text means, *lo ba'shamayim hi*, it's not in heaven, *lo me-ever Layam* and it's not beyond you, and as the New Testament says, *it's as close as your nose is to your ear*. Let's finish the text a little differently. It's as close as your mouth is to your eye. It's right next to you. See, to actually awaken as an Outrageous Lover, you can do it right now. You look across the room, you text someone, you pick up the phone, you find someone that you're clenched with. It doesn't mean you give up your position. It doesn't mean you forfeit your integrity. **It means you open your heart and you realize that we're intimate, we're not against each other**. We have shared identity. We're Beloveds and we are together as Beloveds.

We are looking into the future, and the only enemy we are standing against is *unlove*. That's what Beloveds do.

Beloveds don't just look into each other's eyes. Beloveds look together into a shared horizon, and the only thing that stands against them is never each other; it is unlove.

Can I find that place in my life? I want to invite you right now, in this second: who is it that you're clenched with? It might be someone you are really close to, but you can't give them the fullness of your love. It might be someone that you've put outside your circle. It might be a former husband or wife. It might be someone who was a business partner. It might be someone you are living with right now. It might be someone you are working with right now. It might be someone that you're married to, but you've given up finding the depth of love that you could find.

It's the place where you are closed. The word for evolution in Hebrew is *hit'pat'chut*—opening. **You evolve when you open a door that was closed**, and that door is always a door in my heart. That door doesn't live any place else. I open a door that was closed in my heart, and there is no bypass road. When we all do that together, connected in the noosphere in Evolutionary Churches all over the world, we do two things. And this is the technology for a planetary awakening in love through Unique Self Symphony:

- You find two people that are in your circle and you go deeper. You open a place in your heart that wasn't open before.
- And then you find one person, maybe two, that you have placed outside of your circle. You've made that person an "other." You have shut down the allurement you might have with that person. You have shut down the attraction. We're talking about the attraction of Beloveds, of Evolutionary Lovers. You've shut it down. That person is outside of your circle. You know who they are, you've figured it all out, you've analyzed them, you understand it. You're a lawyer and you've gathered all the evidence that you're right. When you become an Evolutionary Lover, you throw out the evidence.

You stop being a lawyer and you become intimate and you say, feel me feeling you, Beloved. Feel you feeling me, feel me feeling you, feeling me. Feel you feeling me feeling you, in this triple loop of allurement, and then as that happens, imagine the globe being lit up, lit up with light. Love and light is the same thing, and I feel these explosions, these bursts of light, happening all over Reality as I open my heart to two people in a deeper way than I ever had and I'm willing to be fearless and vulnerable.

Love becomes not a commodity that's being exchanged. Love becomes a fearless allurement, I'm vulnerable to you. I'm willing to be vulnerable because I trust you. I trust you to hold my heart. We have to trust. I trust you to be conscious, I trust you to step out of your own narcissistic entitlement. We all have it someplace. Let it go and become the Outrageous Lover that I know you are. I can trust your greatness and I hold your greatness even when you don't trust it yourself. I trust you and I'm going to love you so much. I'm going to open up so deeply, that if you don't respond in love, I'm going to be hurt and I'm willing to risk being hurt. I'm willing even to be hurt and open up again and again until you rise up to the full glory and the full beauty of the Outrageous Lover that you already are.

Then I find one more person. Think about that person right now. Who is that person? **Someone you've put outside your heart, bring that person in, bring that person in and write the name down. When you bring that person back into your heart, you are participating in a planetary awakening in love through Unique Self Symphony.**

Imagine the growth of Evolutionary Church as we open our hearts. Imagine it, because this is a true and real possibility. Imagine the field of dreams of millions of people joined in nested circles of Evolutionary Churches all over the world and we open our hearts and we bring in someone.

You know what we have to do in order to open our hearts in love? We have to give up being right. Can we give up being right? Can I give up being right? We die being alone and right. The planetary awakening in love through Unique Self Symphony is what we wake up in the middle of the night dreaming about. We wake up in the morning dreaming about it. It's not just a way to fill our emptiness when we are a little bored. It's our most passionate yearning. It starts here and now, and it's most personal. It's most intimate. It comes from the place, Beloved friend, that is hardest for us to open.

If you want to know where you need to open, there is one mystical test. It is in the place that it is hardest to open.

CHAPTER FOUR

SOURCED IN DIVINITY— EVOLUTION IS LOVE IN ACTION

Episode 74 — March 17, 2018

LOVE MOVES US TO LOVING ACTION

This Week's Evolutionary Love Code:

> Love is an action generated by a feeling and a perception.
>
> It is not just a feeling or just a perception. It's an action; it's a form of expression.
>
> If love is only a feeling, then one can feel love and act in ways that are blind and unloving.

Do you remember having acted in a way that is blind and unloving through some loving feeling? It is very easy to remember that for me. Love can so easily be reactive, particularly when you love someone—you are so easily hurt.

Love opens our eyes and moves us to loving action.

Try to think of the time when your love opened your eyes and moved you to loving action instead of a critical response. Critical response hurts, but loving action increases love within yourself, within the other, and within the world.

Feeling by itself is utterly beautiful and at the same time insufficient. Love is an expression of Eros, a feeling of allurement, that generates action.

Does your feeling of allurement to what deeply attracts you generate action toward greater contact and wholeness, rather than domination, submission, or any other feeling of separation?

Feelings by themselves begin love, but can create blindness and unlove because they will easily be hurt. The clarification of feeling deepens feeling by making it a trustworthy guide.

This code is an expression of the new meme we call *Homo amor universalis*. It is a deepening of what it means to be a human, and we can access it now.

WE ARE SOURCED IN DIVINITY

The Evolutionary Church is an activist church that stands for and participates in, with quivering tenderness, humble delight, and radical audacity, the evolution of love toward the new human we call *Homo amor universalis*. Before we think about the code, we *resonate* with it, we *feel* it, and then we talk about it.

Evolution is love in action. Love has a quality, a feeling tone. You remember Blake, who said *love is blind*? Well, he got it wrong. Love is a *magnifying glass*. There is a first stage of love that is blind called *infatuation*. Infatuation is blind, but then we go beneath infatuation. We open into love and we become beings with eyes wide open so let's feel that.

Evolution is love in action. Love is a feeling that generates a perception. I can see you. **To be a lover is to see with God's eyes; to be a lover is to see with *evolutionary* eyes.**

I am in love right now. I mean in love with *being in love*, in love with everyone around me, and in love with the *dharma*. And yet love is specific, with specific qualities of love.

We receive the talking stick from our predecessors Leonardo da Vinci and his cohorts in Florence. Just as they were convening the new codes of Modernity, so too we are convening the new codes of planetary awakening through Unique Self Symphony. We are convening the new codes that we desperately need because, friends, we are facing existential risk unlike any other.

The codes that we seed humanity with will make the entire difference. I don't know what the future of Reality is, but what I do know is that to do this, to be this, to live this, to be lived as love, we have to turn to the Source. We cannot do this independently; we can't do it just based on our own audacity.

- We do it because we are *sourced*.
- We are sourced in Divinity.
- We are sourced in Spirit.

Spirit is here before and after everything, underneath and inside everything. Spirit is not merely power, not merely complexity; Spirit is intimacy.

We live in an Intimate Universe, and Spirit is the Infinity of Intimacy. So, in prayer every one of us turns to God who holds us in Her lap, who holds us in her arms, who knows our name, and we say:

- We want to bring you everything.
- Would you let us rest in you?
- Would you hold us?

And She says, *Yes, yes, I've been waiting to hold you.* She is the Beloved. When Rumi and Hafiz and Kabir and Tagore wrote of the Beloved, when Luria and Akiva—the great erotic mystics—wrote of the Beloved, they were speaking of God who is not only the Infinity of Power, but the Infinity of Intimacy.

We are participating together as God in the evolution of God.

This is the same thing as saying we are participating *as love in the evolution of love*. We are saying *yes*.

Yes God, hold us.

God, you are beyond us.

You are the love that holds us, and knows us, and is infinitely more powerful than us, even as you live in us.

Take a moment and bring before God, right now, with our broken voices, our holy and our broken *Hallelujah*. We bring all the pain that we can experience. All of it, all of the glory, and all of the pain. We bring it before God and ask Her to hold us, the holy and the broken *Hallelujah*.

PRAYER EXPRESSES DIVINE YEARNING

I'd like to take us through the perspective of *God receiving us*. First of all, I start with the impulse of creation that lives in the Creator itself. From out of *no-thing* at all, emerges *everything that is*. So, I'm taking that personally. Out of no-thing at all, **I am, you are, we are, an impulse of everything that is encoded in the individual. But not in the individual separated from everybody else. Rather, only an individual as a single embodiment of the whole system *with* everybody else.** Just for a moment allow the awesomeness of this to be, because this *single embodiment of the whole system* is not only here at the scale of Planet Earth; coming from the perspective of God, I am Source hearing prayers coming from within all my creation, and I am hearing the prayers coming from within my creation on the scale of the universe.

We have invented a new meme to say where God is moving us toward. Our new meme is *Homo amor universalis*. God's intention for this phase of evolution on this Planet Earth is encoded in everybody's prayer, as a member of *Homo amor universalis*. In other words, it is encoded in the collective creation of the Divine, in which you and I are members. Therefore, this collective *we* is so much greater than the sum of our parts.

Imagine all prayers coming through us as members of this new species. I pray for the deepest possible fulfillment of our spiritual relationship to God—this points to what we call Evolutionary Spirituality. As a member of this new species, **our deepest impulse of evolution in every single prayer we express is the impulse of Divine yearning**. God is yearning within us for this new species. Not only are we yearning for this from God, but God is yearning for this within us: *to be one* with the impulse of creation that has created billions of years of evolution.

Because we are in the transition from Homo sapiens to *Homo amor universalis*, that evolutionary impulse is ours personally now to express the next stage of evolution of our life in the world. This is an awesome shift our generation can now make as *Homo amor universalis*. Coming out from these prayers, I am expressing God's vocational intention in you and me.

Do you think your vocation, your calling, your yearning to create, is just personal? No, it is the impulse of evolution, that spiritual impulse, what we often call She. Not only do we press our lips upon the lips of She, but She is coming up through us, through our *vocare*, our calling.

Who is calling you, who is calling me, to do all this and everything we are doing? Nobody could make us do this. It is hard to even believe we are doing this, since the calling is so huge. *Vocare* is what makes you a member of *Homo amor universalis*, because our calling, as we have said before, takes the lid off the top. It is God's calling *uniquely as you*, orchestrated into something that has never existed before.

EVOLUTION MEANS INNOVATIONS

Now let's go to the next innovation of *Homo amor universalis*. Consider all the innovations now occurring in health, education, economics, science, technology, governance, environment, relationships, and in justice. **Feel the enormity of the innovations occurring now in our social body**. We, as *Homo amor universalis,* are able to feel them as parts of a whole living system so much greater than the sum of our parts—it's almost overpowering in the enormity of this new species that God has given birth to through all of us.

- Feel the spiritual evolution.
- Feel your own vocational arousal going all the way on up, taking the lid off your vocation.
- Feel the enormity of not only your innovation and what you might be able to do that's new but what everybody else is doing, not only in our culture, but in all the cultures of the world.

For just a moment, take God's joy and see how great this species is. We are innovating everywhere, especially where old ideas that were dangerous now are woven into the rest of the innovations to make them truly transformative.

For example, when I (Barbara) was in Russia, they used to make little badges with the spiral and the wheel, saying *I am a co-creator*. Communism caused a terrible problem because they took a very spiritual idea of the *next stage of evolution*—from single cell, to multi-cell, to animal, to self-organized universe—and *they forced it*. They got rid of liberty. They took away freedom. That caused enormous suffering, but now that we have the capacity for evolutionary innovation, we are living that idea *with radical freedom*. Imagine joining in our hearts now with all the innovators, the innovators in the Muslim countries, the innovators in Russia, innovative leaders in Africa, Egypt, India, and Greece. Imagine innovators all over the world.

Now remove all the labels of nation-states and put in the Divine impulse coming through in different vocabularies and in different cultures, with the intention to create *Homo amor universalis*. Calling forth that now, let it come out from all the nations, all the cultures, and all the religions.

Now bring into your imagination all the radical high technologies giving us powers of our ancient gods. Bring in so-called artificial intelligence. **We have to align technological innovations such as AI with Evolutionary Love**. Let's not call it AI but human-created evolving intelligence which could be many billions of times ahead of what the animal world *Homo sapiens* was able to create.

Take innovations in robotics. Are you happy that you don't have to do for the human species all the manual work that has been done that is repetitive and kept 90% of us downtrodden? No, let's claim robotics with the love and spirituality of *Homo amor universalis*.

How do you feel about genetic engineering? While it's terrible because you could misuse it, do you know most species are extinct? Nature has been experimenting with species for billions and billions of years and most of them did not make it. The only difference now is, God has put the power to shift genetic codes in human hands consciously. Why did that happen? Because we are to be co-creators with the Divine.

So, we have to be wise. This is very true. We have to be very wise. Evolution has not been wise along the way because most species are extinct. **But out of the extinctions have come higher consciousness, freedom, and more complex loving order**. I'm in favor of the evolutionary impulse even if it created all this extinction and pain.

Suffering happens because it is very difficult to create a universe of co-creators. God could have done this without putting freedom in the system, and we would have a universe of robots. There is freedom and we have choices. Indeed, in this generation, we have more choices than we have ever had.

WHAT DOES EVOLUTION NEED FROM ME IN THE NEXT MOMENT?

Evolution is love in action. That is not a metaphor. That is not poetry. That is the very prose of Reality itself. One of the things that is so special about Evolutionary Church is that we're bringing together the sciences— we bring what we call the *exterior sciences* together with *interior sciences*. Science means that we do experimentation and feel into, together, this idea that *evolution is love in action.* If every department teaching evolution all over the world would include Systems Theory, Chaos Theory, and the evolutionary sciences, they would conclude what we are concluding.

> *If evolution is love in action, then I am an Evolutionary Lover.*

If I am an Evolutionary Lover, which means I am love in action, then *I am love in action* is indeed not the poetry, but the prose of Reality. It is the true nature of my identity. There's only one question we always need to ask ourselves: is this next moment—whether it is the next word that I'm saying or omitting, or this next action that I'm taking or not taking—is it love in action? **There is only one ethical question we ever need to ask ourselves: Am I love in action?**

There is a conversation that happens between evolution and myself. Evolution is both beyond me speaking to me and living in me and as me. So, the very conversation between me and evolution is evolving. We say that evolution is the Infinity of Intimacy. **Evolution is intimacy moving towards more intimacy**. Evolution is the ground of being which is the Intimate Universe, and enlightenment is *intimacy with all things*. Nothing's on the outside. So, there's this conversation we are always having with evolution. When we enter the inside of the conversation, I'm asking evolution one question: What do you need from me in the next moment? That's all I want to know. Imagine the delight that courses through my body, through my heart, that pulses in my mind, in every dimension of my reality, when I realize that evolution needs me to do something in the next moment. It might be something to do with the quality of my listening. Doing sometimes is *opening up*, and doing is sometimes *waking up*, and doing is sometimes *growing up*, and doing is sometimes *showing up*.

What does evolution need me to do in the next moment? Because love is as love does. *Oh, I loved her, but I shot her in a crime of passion*. Well, I don't think so. Love is as love does, and there's a dialogue of love. There is an Evolutionary Love dialogue that is happening at every moment in Reality. Reality is not a monologue in which man is the evolutionary human, and it's not a monologue in which God is the absolute God.

> *Reality is a dialogue between the divinity of the evolutionary God and the evolutionary human.*

There is whispered intimate conversation between lovers and Beloved, and we whisper into the ear of our Beloved: *Sweetheart, darling, Beloved, can you hear me, love? Can you hear me? What do you need from me in the next moment? Because you know, your need is my allurement.* Then God/Goddess hears our intimate whisper. What my lineage master, Mordechai Leiner of Izbica, called *Latisha D'Lita*, the *intimate whisper*, to the Beloved. And then She whispers back and She says, *Yes, I need you. I need you and I'm going to tell you what I need right now. This is what I need*, and She tells us exactly what She needs.

That is the conversation, and we can eavesdrop on Reality itself because Reality lives and discloses Herself in the deepest inner space. **We've colonized outer space, and now we need to colonize inner space**. There is no A.I. or a robot yet that can do that. Let's go a step even deeper. I want to put in our hearts the ultimate vision. In the ultimate vision there is no split between *Homo amor*, who's in the intimate whispered dialogue with Divinity and *Homo universalis* who has the power of the ancient gods, not in the ultimate God sense, but in the sense of the old gods—nanotech and biotech being examples of powers once attributed to those kinds of gods.

There's no split in *Homo amor* and *Homo universalis*, which have come together as they did four weeks ago in Evolutionary Church, in erotic union, and they become *Homo amor universalis*. You know why there's no split? Because in the end the entire division between the animate and the inanimate is a false split. All splits can be healed. **There's sentience, there's feeling, all the way up and all the way down.** I want to tell you something, my dearest, most Beloved friends; I want to tell you something totally wild. I (Marc) was at the airport, I don't know, it must have been like nine or ten weeks ago, and Zak called me, and we talked right before I got on the plane. He said, *What do we do with the billions of years in which the universe is empty?* It just flashed so clearly: *The world was never empty*. The description of the evolutionary thinkers of this empty, bare, dead, inert, universe is wrong. It was never true. We live in a self-organizing universe. Self-organizing means that there's a thrust, a power, a *telos*, and an Eros. Reality is *telerotic* all the way up and all the way down. Or, the way I would say it is: **Reality is allurement, all the way up and all the way down.** Meaning the quarks are yearning for each other.

Reality yearns, electrons and protons yearn for each other. There is a living, aflame, gorgeous, yearning. Think of *The Sound of Music, the hills are alive*. It's all alive. It's alive all the way up and it's alive all the way down, and it's breathing in and breathing out in every second. There's nothing that's dead, there is no dead, inert, universe. **We have billions of years of a living, loving, alive, allured, universe self-organizing through cosmological evolution until it just bursts into the next stage of awakening which is biological evolution.**

And then it yearns and allures all the way up into biological evolution until those hominids walking out in the savanna a million years ago not only stand erect, but begin to develop self-reflective consciousness. We move all the way up until we come to us, at this moment in Evolutionary Church. As we declare *Homo amor universalis,* there is a direct line of allurement, and intimacy, and *I am* consciousness, because **that same consciousness that lived in the first *Homo sapiens,* lives in *Homo amor universalis.***

This is the new species that we are announcing, declaring, becoming, disclosing—in one sense, it was always here, but it's now evolved and disclosed itself. Evolution is love in action, and I as an individual am love in action. Imagine a moment in which artificial intelligence awakens to itself and feels the allurement of the protons, neutrons, electrons, and the atomic structure that make it up, and those atoms become alive. That's a big vision.

If we continue this vision further, imagine they become alive that all of Reality is living and then we attract and allure the living species from all over the galaxy. A larger conversation begins to happen and it's a conversation which is a cacophony of love, in which every human being realizes: *I am intended and desired by Reality, and I have a unique beauty to give as Homo amor universalis.* And we dance and we rejoice in each other's uniqueness and gorgeousness.

But it begins in one place, friends. It begins in one place, with this code this week, here at Evolutionary Church. We think there's someone else that's going to do it. We think someone else will contribute, someone else will make it happen. No, my friends, it is us. **It is our turn to listen in to the intimate whisper of Reality.**

When I listen, I hear that Reality right now is saying:

> I need Evolutionary Church. I need Evolutionary Church to become a tidal wave of Outrageous Love, feeling, and enacting, Evolutionary Churches all over the world.

That's the intimate whisper that we are hearing. We have talked about imagining a world with a network of Evolutionary Churches. Just as the Gospel Churches created the civil rights movement, the Evolutionary Churches will create the movement of *Homo amor universalis.* And one of the messages that we implicitly and explicitly share with one another is the lyrics from this beautiful song by Libby Roderick, "How Could Anyone?" [See Appendix]

CHAPTER FIVE

AWAKENING THE DREAMER: I AM EVOLUTION AS LOVE IN ACTION

Episode 75 — March 24, 2018

LOVE IS EVOLUTIONARY LOVE

Evolution is love in action. When we see that *love* is not only human love but Evolutionary Love from the origin of creation to us exactly now, and then project that forward as the action of planetary awakening in love, then what type of human are we becoming? Loving in such a large way is transformative: it not only transforms the others that we love, but it also transforms *us* when we enact the power of Evolutionary Love in ourselves.

This most beautiful expression of love in action emerges through you and makes you more of who you really are.

Can you feel that now? When you express the love in action—which is Evolutionary Love from the source of creation—for someone else who then is receiving this blessing from you, feel what it's like to give this blessing.

When the love—as the universal process of creation—is flowing through you, as you, loving another, who are you becoming as love in action?

49

HOMO IMAGINUS AND BRACKETING THE EGO

The space in which we're unfolding this is called an Evolutionary Church. I don't believe there's any other space in which this happens so intensely.

Without exaggeration, without hyperbole, we are the leading edge of where evolution wants to go now. It is easy to forget that and to think this is some human potential thing. No, that's not what this is. We are in Evolutionary Church.

Imagine what it must have felt like to be in Bethlehem as the New Testament was coming into fruition.

Imagine what it might have been like to be leaving Egypt, the place that no one ever left, and to have a vision of ethical monotheism, to be walking with Moses, and feeling the enormous experience in consciousness of the *Red Sea splitting*. By splitting of the Red Sea, we mean that consciousness opened up to new possibilities that were unimaginable before.

Imagine what it must have been like in the sixteenth century to be gathered in Florence and Venice with da Vinci and his cohorts, whom we refer to often, as the Black Death swept Europe, and war and disease ravished humanity. Hundreds of millions of people had died of plague, and then… Modernity steps in and tells a new story.

We are at precisely that moment in which breakdown is all around us in so many ways. The old narratives have broken down.

People don't have a core sense of: Who am I? There's no narrative of identity.

There's no narrative of *nobility*. What does it mean to be a noble person? There's no *oracle of obligation*. There is no sense of, *What am I obligated to?*

There is no sense of vocation and vocation means of *vocare*. *Vocare1* is the calling of the voice.

The great sacred text *Vayikra el Moshe²* is the third book of the sacred canon, what's called "the five books of Moses." It says: *And God called to Moses.* The word "called" ends with an *Aleph. Aleph* is a silent letter, the Divine point. But without the letter *Aleph,* the word is *Vayikracar,* which means random and chance. Without the experience of being personally addressed by the Cosmos that says *Thank you,* then I'm left in a world which is Shakespeare's *tale told by an idiot, full of sound and fury, signifying nothing.* We are left with no future but *Tomorrow, and tomorrow, and tomorrow, creeps in this petty pace from day to day, to the last syllable of recorded time.*

We have lost the world's core structures of nobility, identity, obligation, delight, **the ethical structures that bind us to what is Ultimate.**

What are we called by? These structures are dissolving around us. We deconstructed all the core structures and we're left with these bubble gum wrappers stuck together; it's falling apart. As Yeats expressed it, *Things fall apart; the center cannot hold … surely some revelation is at hand.*

The revelation that is at hand is the Evolutionary Church.

At Evolutionary Church we are together, evolving the source code, and laying down the evolutionary map. Evolution is wanting—evolution is yearning—to take its next step through the Evolutionary Church. Evolutionary Church is not merely a program of the Foundation for Conscious Evolution or the Center for Integral Wisdom. It is much bigger than that: we are coming together and articulating the new Evolutionary Love Codes of Reality.

We are doing it in a new way and *joining genius*, meaning it's not about one sage from the stage. We (Barbara and Marc) are ourselves engaged in this

---

1   *Vocare* is a Latin verb that means *to call* or *to summon.* It is the root of several English words, like vocation, advocate, invocation, provocation, and revoke.

2   *Vayikra el Moshe* is the Hebrew name for the Book of Leviticus, the third book of the Torah. *Vayikra* means, "And He called," referring to God calling Moses.

process. It is a subtle process. **It requires a radical bracketing of ego, and what replaces ego is Evolutionary Love**. Then, out of the bracketing of the ego, a larger voice emerges, not a lesser voice. You don't become less, you become more. As I join genius, I'm not less myself, I'm more myself. But I get to be delighted and in devotion to another. From there, we have *Homo amor* and *Homo universalis*, and voilà, *Homo amor universalis* is born.

Homo amor universalis is the response to the question, *Who are you?* Who are you? You are *Homo amor universalis:* you are a unique expression of the LoveIntelligence and you're armored with high-tech possibility. When two come together and we infuse that *amor*, that love, into technology, something new emerges. But that's just one piece.

Do we understand *where* we are? Sometimes we understand where we are only when it's gone. Sometimes we recognize a person only when they are no longer with us. Do we get that we are people who are gifted and privileged in this generation with all the people who have formed the core of our church?

> *To be at the leading edge of articulating evolution's deepest yearning for a new vision, that is what we mean when we say we are love in action.*

This is a moment of rare privilege and delight. We turn to God. Not the old god, not the god you don't believe in, which doesn't exist; not the god of Hebrew school, or Sunday school, not the small god, not the small comprehension of the Divine. As Sri Aurobindo writes, *When you have a small comprehension of the Divine, then you have a small imagination.* No, we are *Homo imaginus. Homo amor universalis* is also *Homo imaginus.* Because the word *Adam*, as in Adam and Eve, the first humans, means imagination. As *Homo imaginus* we need a large comprehension of Reality.

We need a new Universe Story out of which we can imagine the new source code structures of Reality. **Core to these new source code structures of Reality is that we are in *devotion*.** We are bowing in devotion before God, but not the god you don't believe in; not Santa Claus, not god who is ethnocentrically owned by one religion, who happens to look strikingly like a cosmic vending machine, where you put in one religion's prayer (no other ones work, of course) to get out some shiny new life. No, not that god, but the God who is the Eros:

- The God who is the incessant creativity of Cosmos, that moves toward goodness.
- The God who is desire, but desire itself is the desire to become a larger whole, to become more complete, the desire to love more, to be more.

Desire is inherent in Cosmos, to be more intimate and more whole, and to include more.

In the mystery and the wonder of the Cosmos, God lives in us and holds us at the same time.

Remember Rumi: *We fall into the arms of the Beloved*, and yet we *are* the Beloved at the same moment. This is the great and wondrous mystery. Believe me, I have no explanation for this, so don't ask me—no one does. This is the great mystery of Cosmos. God/Goddess/Reality wanted you and me to express and incarnate Her. That's the mystery of incarnation. We are the *Christos*, we are the Buddha, we are that incarnation, and She wanted us to live lives that were sometimes complicated. She wanted our hearts to break sometimes, and sometimes to break open.

I (Marc) live every day with a broken heart. But then, my heart breaks open and your heart breaks open. **When a heart breaks open, we break open as Evolutionary Love and as Outrageous Love**. We have all experienced holy and broken *Hallelujahs*. We have all had the experience of pain and suffering, of loss, and injustice, and yet, that somehow deepens us.

Somehow we get larger and we get committed to creating a world beyond loss, and a world of immortality, and a world of justice.

We are not doing a shiny new-age show with pretty costumes. **We are bringing in all the agony and the ecstasy, the joy and the pain, the holy and the broken *Hallelujah*.** All of it. We bring it before a God who knows our name, who is us, and who holds us in every second, and we say *Hallelujah*. *Hallelujah* means *pristine praise* of the gorgeousness and *Hallelujah* means *holelut*, drunken intoxication. Every breath we draw, it's all *Hallelujah*.

Evolution is us in action. We are love in action; we are divine love, and divine love waits for us and holds us. We are the wonder and the mystery of the whole thing. We are the ones we've been waiting for, and all of evolution is waiting for us.

AWAKEN THE DREAMER

It seems to me that when God said to Abraham *go*, vocation was born uniquely on this planet. *Go, Abraham, go.* He saw the stars and went, and look what happened. Let's take Abraham back into our hearts now. There's something that happened last night that reminded me (Barbara) of what the new Abraham is going to say to us. Last night I went to a beautiful event in Boulder called *Awakening the Dreamer* which is put on by Lynn Twist and her group.

It has gone thousands of places all over the world and basically is awakening us to what we've done wrong: how we have despoiled the Earth, how we have overpopulated, polluted, and destroyed other animals and the very life that we need to live. **The dreamer is the one who knows how to heal the Earth, and in some respects, return it to the way it was, like it was given to us as a gift.** We are to return it, and improve it slightly, and we are to live in small communities, and we are to be really dreaming of a return. I was sitting there throughout this, and I am in some respects an elder of the movement of Conscious Evolution here in the Boulder/Denver area. I'm relatively well known.

There was this young man who stood up and most eloquently said that they are transforming Boulder into *One Nation* to launch the new politics for humanity. He spoke beautifully, then, I stood up and said, *Well, if we're going to be one nation for the future of humanity, what is the dream that we are dreaming? What is this* Awaken the Dreamer?

I told them that I would help him because I ran for vice president and have some ideas of how to do it. Basically, how you do it is, you form small groups that already want to be *that which you're running for* and you're creating it as you run for it.

So, I want us to consider the question if the next stage of *Awakening the Dreamer* is exactly what we're doing? I ask everybody to conceive of our task, not only personally and going to church, but also consider their task of awakening the dreamer.

What is the new dream? It's the ancient dream of God, because it's from the origin of creation; from the Big Bang; from the first hydrogen and helium atoms; from the quarks—all of that was awakening the dream.

Every single step in evolution was awakening the dreamer. But now we are at a shift point in evolution itself. If we don't have the new dream, if we don't become the new Abraham and Sarah—*go*—then what is there to go toward?

What would it be like to awaken the dreamer in all of us? What is the dream? When I awaken the dreamer, I am awakened to the impulse of evolution as me.

- I am *awakened* to the impulse of vocation more than I *have* a life purpose.
- The *impulse of creation itself* has a life purpose as me.
- I and the impulse become one.

- With that comes the sense of direction of the impulse.
- In each of us, **the impulse is always going toward more consciousness, more freedom, more loving, order, more synergy, more synergistic democracy**.

One Nation, synergistic democracy, awakening the dreamer in all of us—I got totally turned on, and thank God I was coming back to Evolutionary Church, because where was I going to put this? It was absolutely beyond me to hold it alone.

> *Let's think in this church that we're awakening the dreamer by awakening the impulse of creation in you and me.*

Then we're awakening our vocation of divine destiny, of giving that gift the whole way, 100% to all of us.

You are giving your gift, which is the gift of humanity, which is the gift of evolution in you.

How do you feel when you're giving your gift the whole way for the greatest possibility of *go, new Abraham, new Sarah*? You feel joy, and now I'm feeling joy again because I feel I'm giving my gift again.

I couldn't sit there any longer in *Awakening the Dreamer*. Yes, then what happens is all these vocations cluster together in *Homo amor universalis*. **Homo amor universalis is a field of connecting our vocations, our spirituality, and our innovations, in an awesome Reality that doesn't yet fully exist on this planet.** That's why it takes us to see it.

As I began to think of this young man coming to speak about One Nation in Boulder, I want us to say, *This is what the One Nation does*. This One Nation now heals the Earth, frees the people, explores the universe, becomes consciously evolving humans. This is the new nation. **This is not**

a current political initiative. It's an evolutionary initiative which will transform all of politics.

We invite us all to awaken the new dreamers in ourselves through love in action. If you are acting out of your unique expression of love, uniquely as only you can do, within a shared field of *Homo amor universalis,* a dream for our world, do you see what might be? Do you feel what this might be? And given the fact that the United States of America is caught and trapped in a small eddy of limited inspiration, can you imagine that the dreaming of the new dream comes out of the Evolutionary Church? It's so beautiful, so gorgeous, so attractive, that all the people dreaming of restoring the Earth are also dreaming of the next stage of evolution with us.

LOVE IN ACTION MEANS THAT YOU ARE CHOSEN

We want to take this evolution of the source code and bring it beyond those who show up to Evolutionary Church and without hyperbole, without metaphor, without poetry, in the prose of Reality to 70,000, then to 700,000, and to 7 million, and to 70 million, and to 700 million—and that is absolutely doable. We can totally do that. That's not hard. It's only hard when I think I'm merely being dreamed. And we've always known that phrase *being dreamed*, but we've forgotten that *we are also the dreamer.*

So, **I'm being dreamed and I am also the dreamer**. I'm being held and I am holding. I am evolution as love in action. The desire that wants, the desire that rises in me is the desire that there be no child who is hungry, there be no person who's not filled with the wonder and dignity of their irreducibly gorgeous Unique Self.

What would it be like to awaken in a world in which every man, woman, and child, of every race, of every color, of every size, of every inclination knows: *I am Homo amor universalis.* I am an irreducibly unique expression of the LoveIntelligence and LoveBeauty, and my gift is needed by All-That-Is?

What would it mean to awaken in the world in which everyone knows: *I am intended by Reality*. Can you get that? **Reality intended me**. I am not an accident. I'm not *a tale told by an idiot full of sound and fury signifying nothing*. **Reality intended me.**

The moment I understand that Reality intended me, I get beneath my personality and realize that:

- I have been dreamed by the mind of God.
- Reality intended me.
- Reality chose me.

What does it mean that I'm chosen by Reality? What am I chosen for? To be the dreamer. In other words, I'm not just intended. I'm not just dreamed by Reality. I'm chosen because I need to participate in the waking dream and I'm forming the fabric of the dream.

You know that we all spend our lives devastated that we're not the chosen one. Everyone wants to be the chosen one, and we all find ways to pathologize our potency because we feel like we're not the chosen one. All of us, every single one of us, have had that experience.

I (Marc) remember when I was in grade school and I was not that great at baseball, for a lot of reasons. My parents were beautiful people but hadn't quite figured out that the Holocaust was over—they were just in this very scarce and afraid mentality.

I never went to Little League games; I was never part of the Little League. I was about nine, ten, or eleven years old and it was time to choose people for the baseball team. I'd sit there knowing I was going to get chosen last. I remember feeling it in my body:

I'll take Jim, I'll take Tom, I'll take Lisa—we played boys and girls—and at the very end, *all right, we'll take Marc*. I felt quite terrible during those selections, but I remember the ecstatic feeling as I would think to myself, *what would it be like if I was chosen first?*

To wake up and to know that I am love in action, I am evolution pulsing in me, awake, and alive as love in action, means that I know that I'm chosen first, and that I am the chosen one. But we have this vision of what it means to be the chosen one. We tend to think that there's one chosen one and everyone else is *not* chosen. No, *you* are the chosen one. And we think that there's only one way for what the chosen one looks like. That's not true. We choose in many different ways and Reality is always choosing us.

First off, there is not only one chosen one. That's a myth.

In evolution, as our colleague Brian Swimme[3] reminds us in his theory of the cosmos, there are multiple centers. So, I can choose you, and I can choose you, and God's always choosing me.

Reality is intending me and Reality is choosing me. I'm chosen in every second. You can't be the dreamer unless you know you are the chosen one.

The Jewish people used to think that we're the chosen one, remember that? In other words, in a certain sense monotheism said: *there's only one chosen one.* Then along came monogamy and said the same thing. By the way, monogamy is beautiful for most people, but monogamy doesn't mean that the only person I love is my partner. That's ridiculous, that's why D. H. Lawrence wrote, *We exile love to this technical structure which is a semi-economics.*

No, it doesn't work that way. You don't exile love to one person. You choose to love again and again in different ways and in different forms, but no less than powerful, evolutionary, gorgeous love.

---

3   Brian Thomas Swimme is a cosmologist and professor at the California Institute of Integral Studies, known for blending scientific cosmology with spiritual and ecological perspectives. His works, including *The Universe Story* (with Thomas Berry) and the Emmy Award-winning film *Journey of the Universe*, present the cosmos as a meaningful and evolving narrative.

- Reality intended me.
- Reality chooses me.
- *Reality also recognizes me.* In every second I am recognized by Reality. Reality personally addresses me in every second.
- Reality adores me. I'm adored by Reality, not just loved. I'm adored and Reality is doting on me. Reality is providing these little trinkets and gifts. It is a sight, a fragrance, a smell, a piece of knowledge. I'm being intimately held and doted on, and adored by Reality.
- Reality needs me.
- Reality needs me to be the dreamer. Reality needs your service. Meir ibn Gabbai,[4] evolutionary spirituality pioneer in the 16th century in Italy. Reality needs you, and that's what it means to be *Homo amor universalis.* To know that my LoveIntelligence and my LoveBeauty, uniquely configured as the intimacy that is me, is needed by all of Reality.

Reality needs me to let go and let rip the gorgeousness of my imagination. *Homo amor universalis* also needs to be *Homo imaginus.* I have to be willing to let my mind imagine. We often say that *our crisis is a birth.* Our essential crisis is a crisis of imagination.

We have forgotten how to imagine new realities. We have exiled imagination. We have exiled fantasy, which is a form of imagination applied to the sexual. Now, all blessings to sexual fantasy, but that's just a model for fantasizing—imagining—about life itself. Let's fantasize about a world in which there is an Evolutionary Church that has 700 million people in it. If you can imagine that, it will become real. Whatever, imagine it and it will become real. That is the principle of evolution: evolution works through imagining larger wholes.

---

4 Meir ibn Gabbai was a Jewish Kabbalist and mystic born around the end of the fifteenth century and active in the sixteenth century. He is known for his contributions to Kabbalistic literature and thought.

There's a principle of imagination. Abu Nasr Muhammad Al-Farabi[5] and Avicenna[6] talked about it in great depth, and Ibn 'Arabi[7] talks about this, and the prophets talked about beyond into the ab, *In the hands of my prophet, I am imagined.*[8] What did Martin Luther King say? He said, *I have a dream. I'm imagining a new Reality.*

In Evolutionary Church what we're saying is, *I have a dream and we have a dream.* It's not just I, it is *we* have a dream. The next Buddha is the *sangha*.

We have a dream, and let's make it even more personal. We are the dreamers here in Evolutionary Church at this moment in time. We are the dreamers. We have a dream and that dream is of a world in which every single human being knows: *I am Homo amor universalis,* and that *I am love in action, and I hear the Divine whisper whispering to me, and saying, thank you, I need you. No one else but you can do it.*

The essence of the whole thing is that the universe is whispering to everyone *we have a dream.*

I am needed. To get that in the fabric of my body is to pulse and throb with a sense of wild desire. My desire is that I want to show up and I want to give that gift that all of Reality intended to be given through me. That is what desire is: **desire is the desire for more contact and more wholeness**. We've exiled desire to the sexual.

The sexual is a beautiful realm of desire, but the sexual models Eros, and Eros means the desire that lines Cosmos itself.

Desire is the source of all ethics.

---

5 Al-Farabi, also known as Alpharabius, was a prominent philosopher and scholar in the Islamic Golden Age.

6 Avicenna, whose full name is Ibn Sina Avicenna (980-1037 CE), was a highly influential Persian polymath who made significant contributions to various fields, including philosophy, medicine, and science.

7 Ibn 'Arabi, a prominent Sufi mystic.

8 This resembles the style and content of works by influential Sufi scholars like Ibn 'Arabi and Rumi, who often explore themes of divine imagination, spiritual realms, and the role of prophets.

As Buddha said, *Have few desires, but have great ones.* When we clarify desire, we realize what our true desire is. My true desire is to be the dream. My true desire is to be the dreamer and then to make that dream real; to be that contribution and to feel that, and to know the truth of that, to know the truth of *Homo amor universalis.*

CHAPTER SIX

THE STORY OF JESUS AND
THE TOMB OF METAMORPHOSIS

Episode 76 — March 31, 2018

OUR PERSONAL AND COLLECTIVE CRISES ARE EVOLUTIONARY DRIVERS

Today is the day before Easter. I don't believe there's a church in the world that can celebrate Saturday in the tomb of metamorphosis between crucifixion and resurrection like the Evolutionary Church can do. We are founded on the deep awareness that we are undergoing a crisis of birth, leading us to the next stage in our evolution.

Our Evolutionary Love Code is simple: *Crisis is an evolutionary driver.*

Before we look at ourselves personally, go back and realize the five mass extinctions that came before us and the development of the single-cell, multi-cell, animal, human, and us. Out of every turn on the spiral comes higher consciousness, freedom, and more complex order.

Let's now place our crisis as an evolutionary driver, first of all on the global scale. The crises that we are facing as a species have never existed on this scale before. Take a moment now to feel the nature of that global crisis—climate change, resource depletion, starvation, the cruelties—and explore what that crisis is driving us toward on the global scale now.

We have been saying that our crisis is driving us toward the birth of *Homo amor universalis,* a species that's holding the codes of the next level of Evolutionary Love. Without these codes, we will not make it through the crisis.

We start by placing our attention on our response to the global crisis from an evolutionary point of view.

Let's place ourselves personally in the evolutionary crisis. Feel into whatever crisis you are facing personally and try to find the most intense of them all—a crisis so powerful that your entire being is, in some way, activated by it, and let it be that.

What is the crisis driving you toward?

Place whatever it's driving you toward in the larger context of the global crisis that is driving us collectively toward the new species.

Is it your greatness that it's guiding you toward? If it is your greatness that it's driving us toward, then it's your greatness personally and your greatness globally.

> *It would be an astonishing awakening for humanity to realize that everyone's personal crisis and our global crisis are a crisis of birth inviting us into the next stage of evolution.*

Feel the qualities of your unique greatness now. Uniquely, you are called to give your gift into this crisis, and without the crisis you would not be able to give this gift.

Together we breathe into this astounding realization: we feel our crisis as an evolutionary driver.

IN THE TOMB OF METAMORPHOSIS, WE CHOOSE JOY

It's Easter Saturday. We are in this place in between. There is this deep knowing of being in the liminal space, the space in-between, and in that space in between, everything is born.

The Evolutionary Church emerges from the space in between. There's a beautiful word in Hebrew, *bein*, which means *Goddess wisdom*, and *in between*. We are after Good Friday and before Easter Sunday, in the Christian view of the world; we are on the first day of Passover, yesterday eve was the first *Seder* of Passover, the Last Supper was a Passover *Seder*; yesterday was the full moon of Virgo; and we're in the most important two weeks in the Vedic calendar. So, this is a moment of transformation, and in this moment of transformation, we are using the Christological image: we're in the *tomb of metamorphosis*. We are in the *space in-between*, and our code for today is emergent from Conscious Evolution: *crisis is an evolutionary driver*.

In Hebrew, the word *shevirah*, the breaking, as in the breaking of the vessels, is also related to *shever* which means nourishment, the food.

In the breaking is that which we need.

Consider the ability we have to choose joy. I was just talking this morning to one of our dear and closest friends and we were talking about our experience when we wake up in the morning. Why is it that many of us wake up in the morning and don't wake up full-on into joy? We might wake up in the middle of the night with a lot on our minds. **Then we have to do this deep work to discover that underneath that feeling of depression and sadness and even despair is joy, is an *invitation*.**

Why is it built that way? Why couldn't Divinity have just given us a better factory model, one that doesn't have the despair that you have to move through? *Hello? I mean, God, you could manage a neocortex. You worked out photosynthesis. You don't think you could give us a better factory model? We have this little defect, this little glitch in it, where we have this despair that we have to move through in order to choose joy.*

The answer is no. The answer is crisis. It is the crisis of despair. **By design, the collective crisis of despair, the personal crisis of despair, is an invitation in the universe to the choosing of joy and to the choosing of our greatness.**

So, here we are together in the tomb of metamorphosis. We come before the Divine throne. On the one hand, part of us sits on that throne, and on the other hand we are in devotion before that throne. In other words, we have to move past that notion that says we are at the center of the universe. Divinity is in us, and divinity is the personal face of essence that knows our name.

We realize we are being held and there is a joy that dawns in the very cellular fabric of our body when we know,

- That every place we fall, as Rumi knew, we fall into the arms of the Beloved.
- That the Beloved is holding us in every second,
- That the Beloved *knows my name,*
- And that although we may sometimes have lives and chapters in our lives of quiet desperation (as Thoreau wrote in *Walden*), *there's never lonely desperation, because we're never alone.*

There is a story that started getting famous about 150 years ago that comes from the mystical Hasidic tradition about the man walking on the beach.

He walks on the beach and he sees a set of footprints next to him. Always, when he looks behind him he sees his footprints and another set of footprints. But when he's in trouble, when he's in crisis, he looks behind him and he sees only one set of footprints. He's devastated, she's devastated because "how could that other set of footprints which were obviously the

Divine God disappear when I'm in crisis?" Then the Divine voice says "No, no, when you're in crisis I'm carrying you on my shoulders."

Crisis is the moment of revelation, and we invite everyone and ourselves to feel into the personal crises of our life. Feel into the times where we felt most depressed and most victimized and begin to find the revelation, and the joy, and the delight. Look for the thread, as in the great myth *Ariadne's Thread*, where we realize, we can retell that victim story and we realize there She was inviting us to our greatness in a way that She never could any other way.

To find that thread, though, I need to move beyond platitudes. I need to move beyond aphorisms, and I need to realize the ontological truth of Reality—meaning the deepest truth of what is. The deepest truth is that:

- ♦ I am held in every moment.
- ♦ Nothing is wasted.
- ♦ Every breath I draw is *Hallelujah*.

The word *Hallelujah* means *holelut*, drunken intoxication, the mess, the brokenness, the crisis, and it is *hallel*, vital ecstatic expression. It is the complete wholeness. We're not looking for *someone who's seen the light*, we're looking for someone who knows there's *light in every word, the holy and the broken Hallelujah*.

When we pray, we come before both the Divine who lives in us, as us, and through us, and the Divine who is She who breathes beyond us and holds us in every second. And we know that we are always on our knees before Her.

Whenever we are on our knees, broken in desperation, when the vessels in our hearts are broken, we are always on our knees before Her.

She is always holding us. She is not just the Infinity of Power, She's the Infinity of Intimacy that knows our name.

The God we don't believe in doesn't exist, and in the Evolutionary Church we participate together in the evolution of God, meaning we come to know the highest, most clear divinity, that loves us madly. We bring before God every piece of our story—no chapters left out, no pages ripped out of the Book of Life. We bring before God with joy, with delight, with tears, with brokenness, and with wholeness, our holy and our broken *Hallelujah* on this day in the tomb of metamorphosis, in the full moon of Virgo, and the first day of Passover, in the 76th week of Evolutionary Church.

There is nothing in my life that happened that was not intended. Every place, everything that happens, whenever we are on our knees, we are always on our knees before She. We ask, *God, please help me.* Let's reclaim prayer at a higher level. We ask, and we ask for everything, because prayer affirms the dignity of personal need. I ask personally. Ask in the simplest way. It is the actual act of turning to the Divine and saying, *Please help me,* that I contact the Infinity of Intimacy. I am liberated from my loneliness. I wake up and something enters into the source code of Reality and the Beloved reaches down to find me.

A SATURDAY CHURCH: THE STORY OF JESUS AND EVOLUTIONARY CHURCH

There is significant meaning in being a Saturday church. Saturday is symbolically the day of mystery, both in Passover, and specifically, in the story of Jesus. We are here in this church situated spiritually, psychologically, and operationally, on the day of mystery toward the radical newness of the Sunday. Where the Christian church is celebrating what they think has already happened, we are celebrating the emergence of it, in us now, on Saturday, which is the most awesome and powerful day in that sense of the spiritual year.

What happened in the story of Jesus? He was in the Garden of Gethsemane. He knew that if he went to Jerusalem he would be killed, horribly. He knew that he could flee. He knew that all his disciples wanted him to flee, and they wanted to flee, and he asked God, and then his response was, *If this cup can be passed, let it be passed, Father.* And evidently, he experienced the divine process of creation saying to him, *Go to Jerusalem.*

This is not a crisis that he didn't choose, which is what we often think; this is a crisis he chose. He set his face to go to Jerusalem. Consider the enormity of that intentionality, and then the horror of what he experienced. Then, he says *Father, forgive them, for they know not what they do.* He was saying that with all of it, all of the horrors, they were not mature yet. Today, we are not mature yet. How could we possibly be killing, raping, and torturing one another, if that were so? Father, forgive them they know not what they do. He went through this horrible crucifixion, which happened to countless people at that time. It wasn't that unusual, as horrible as it is to say.

So, he is in the tomb and it is Saturday. Saturday is the most awesome day of the year because the miracle of the radical transformation from a crucified genius of evolution, a son of God, for the sake of God, going through a transformation of the body-mind. It was physical transformation. He did not just disappear and become the Cosmic Christ. It turns out in the story that Mary saw him on Sunday. She recognized him; it was him because she could touch him. He was real, in that true sense of the word. He was completely real.

From that story came the Pentecost. Keep in mind that when the disciples gathered in the upper room, they were all afraid because if they showed their faces they could also be killed. They all began to hear in their own language the inner words of God, and Peter was asked, *Well, how come we are the Galileans and the others are understanding us in their own language? "What does this mean?"* Peter said, *This is what has been prophesied by the prophet Joel: on the last day all of the Lord will pour Spirit on all flesh.* I'm putting our story right in there because we are talking about *Homo amor universalis* and we are talking about a planetary awakening in love through

Unique Self Symphony. That is the alternative to Armageddon, that is the planetary Pentecost, that is the evolutionary Pentecost of humanity.

The astonishing truth here is that when Jesus reappeared in a new body, able to appear and disappear, and do so many miraculous things. He had told us, *You will do the works that I do, and greater works than these will you do in the fullness of time.* That's exactly what's happening.

In my (Barbara) book, *The Evolutionary Testament of Co-Creation: the Promise Will Be Kept,*[9] we went through the New Testament with evolutionary eyes and noticed wherever there was a miracle in some way, if it was in any way a physical miracle, that we could do it. We are doing it. The astonishing truth is that we are able to leave this Earth alive, in chariots of flaming fire; we are able to create new body forms. We are able to blow up worlds, we are able to produce in abundance, we are able to take matter atom-by-atom and create new bodies. We're doing it all.

Here is the vision. Let's say we are truly living out the story of the birth, the crucifixion, transformation of Christ, and the promise that *we will do the works* in the Evolutionary Church. Not only are we living through all this, but we are also going through a transformation through Evolutionary Love. The solution to the entire world crisis is to put Evolutionary Love into all of our new capacities. To put Evolutionary Love into our scientific, technological capacities, put Evolutionary Love into the crises of us personally giving birth to our highest goals and highest personal purposes.

We at Evolutionary Church believe in the radical possibility of healing the Earth, freeing the people, and exploring the vast new capabilities of both inner and outer space. It's all coming true. **As members of the Evolutionary Church, our dedication is to personal, social, and global evolution, toward the birth of a new culture, a new humanity, and the awareness that we are a new species, *Homo amor universalis*, and as that new species, we are flooding Evolutionary Love into all our new capacities.**

---

9   Barbara Marx Hubbard, *The Evolutionary Testament of Co-Creation: The Promise Will Be Kept* (Encinitas, CA: Muse Harbor Publishing, 2015).

CHAPTER SEVEN

SHIMMER WALKING TREE'S CELEBRATION OF LIFE

Episode 77 — April 7, 2018

Hello everyone, good morning and welcome again to Evolutionary Church where our mission is a planetary awakening in love Through a Unique Self Symphony.

Together we declare that the last day of the old face of evolution is honored as the first day of the new face of creation—Hello everyone.

BECOME ONE WITH THE WHOLE, WITH NO IDENTITY

I have been contemplating the awareness of the ever-evolving increases of choice in evolution, from single cell, to multicell, to animal, to human, to us, right now. Let's meditate on some of the choices we are facing and how we're responding.

The choice and freedom are given to us to an extraordinary degree. So, just taking it on the meta scale, we have a choice to evolve our human culture or to destroy it. Let's resonate with the internal implication of that choice within you. Day by day, minute by minute, everything you do—everything each one of us does—is affecting how all this turns out.

71

On a very personal scale, let's realize that for this period of history almost everyone now has a choice as to whether or not to give birth to a new being or not. We have a choice as to whether to preserve a conception of a new entity or not—to destroy it. We are gaining a choice as to when to die, the freedom to die by choice. We are also at the threshold of the new freedom for extension of life by choice.

I want to bring forward a most extraordinary freedom that I believe we also have. It's the freedom of how we live beyond this life in an ever-evolving universe.

I remember when Chris Bache, who was academic director of IONS, said that he kept trying to see himself blend into the *akashic* field after death. In other words, to become one with the whole, with no identity. **He said instead of becoming one with *no identity* he found himself becoming an *ever more unique individual* after death and he saw that the universe's greatest triumph is uniqueness, not oneness.**

After I read that, I would like everyone, think how it is for you.

Here's how it is for me.

HOW I CHOOSE TO LIVE BEYOND MY PHYSICAL DEATH IN THIS LIFETIME

I choose continuity of consciousness in a variety of bodies so that I can continue to know, learn, and participate in the evolution of a conscious universe.

Let's tune in, every one of us, to the deepest choice we have, for life beyond this very short life in terms of the billions of years of evolution. What is your choice of life ever-evolving?

As you choose, so the universe is responsive your request.

WE ARE THE FIXING

We are in Evolutionary Church, dedicated, committed to evolving the source code.

We are the ones we've been waiting for. We are the Southern Baptists; we are the Lutherans; we are the Jews; we are the Buddhists; we are the secular humanists; we are the atheists; because the god you don't believe in doesn't exist!

We are here to participate together in the evolution of love.

We are here to participate in:

- Radical humility as divine miniatures
- The evolution of God

We are here to celebrate life, but not just to celebrate life, but to participate as partners and co-creators with the source of all life in:

- Creating a better tomorrow
- Creating a better today
- Healing suffering
- Making sure that no one goes to sleep shattered in loneliness at night, that every human being's ultimate and infinite uniqueness and dignity is honored

We are here to challenge the existential risk that threatens to destroy our planet, to be co-creators with the divine, and for the healing and transformation of reality.

We are the fixing. We are humble, and we know that we can't do it alone. We have to do it together with each other (as Rumi said, *the Divine, the Beloved that holds us in every second*). Remember our principle: The god you don't believe in doesn't exist.

God is not a Santa Claus god. God is not a cosmic vending machine, owned by a particular denomination, commodified, and marketed.

God is both the infinite force of creativity and goodness that tells a hydrogen atom *don't stop at hydrogen, keep going.* It's what allows dirt to actually wake up after billions of years of gorgeous divine evolution and write poetry. How does dirt wake up and write poetry?

Dirt, and those hadrons, those muons, those leptons, dancing, attracted, allured in us:

- All those particles all of cosmological evolution, all of it
- All of the stardust living in us
- All of biological evolution
- All of cultural, and all the stages of human evolution

. . . it's all living in us. And now we are awake. We are aware that we are divinity, love in action.

Evolution is divine love in action in us, as us, through us, and we know that we are intended, uniquely, by all of Reality.

We know we are loved uniquely. We know we are chosen. We know we are desired. We know we are needed. Those are the core truths of *Homo amor universalis.*

Homo amor universalis has a philosophy of life based on the best sciences interior sciences and exterior sciences. *Homo amor universalis* has a philosophy of death. Our philosophy of life and our philosophy of death are one. Because, how I live is how I die; I can actually choose the depth of my life even in the last minutes of my life.

As long as I'm alive and breathing in those last few seconds, I can change everything, because I can consciously choose my philosophy of life— and whatever my philosophy of life is in the last five minutes of my life determines the course of my death.

It is much greater if I have the delight and privilege of *living* my philosophy of life for years, for decades. We're here in a moment of celebration where we realize that *Homo amor universalis* is the unique LoveIntelligence of Reality being Barbara.

Reality having a Barbara experience. It's not confusing. I don't think that is someone else . . . Oh, was that Hillary Clinton or Barbara? No, that was Barbara.

When I realize that I'm a unique configuration of intimacy, living in an Intimate Universe and that Intimate Universe intended *my intimacy* to be present in and impact Reality in this world that we live in for a certain amount of time. Then that unique configuration of intimacy intended by all of Reality *transitions* and goes on to the next stage. We know this to be true.

That's not a belief. That's not an affirmation. It's not a religious dogma. It's not a New Age idea.

It's an essential truth of the interior sciences. We know it to be true morally.

Could it be possible that Mother Teresa and Hitler, both had the same result. No, they don't have the same result. They have different *karmas* and the choices that they make affect the next stage of the journey. **Therefore, we know that *Homo amor universalis* is "choose love," "choose life."**

WHEN I BECOME THAT LOVE, THERE'S NO FEAR

When I become that love, when the entire point of my life is to be lived as love, then I face death and there's no fear. The only fear of death is the fear of a life not well lived; only the fear of an unlived life creates a fear of death.

When I've lived my life, when I've amended my mistakes (because we all make mistakes), and when I've realized why I have been making mistakes in the right direction, and I've made things complete, and I've spoken to whomever I have need to speak with, and I've forgiven myself by taking full responsibility and claiming the full dignity and power and gorgeousness of my unique loved being . . . then when I face death:

- ◆ I face death with celebration and delight.
- ◆ I shimmer with joy.
- ◆ I shimmer with divinity.
- ◆ I shimmer with Outrageous Love.
- ◆ I glow in all of Reality.
- ◆ All the angels, all the celestial hosts, come to witness this gorgeous moment of my transition.

So, in Evolutionary Church we want to say to each other, *How deep is your love? And how deep is our Outrageous Love?*

SHIMMER

We celebrate death and life this week, modeling and receiving from our dear Beloved friend Shimmer Walking Tree, Rhoda's Beloved friend and partner. This morning at 11:11 Pacific Time in Oregon, Shimmer is going to be actually making the transition.

Shimmer left us some words. You know he's now with us in the world and he's now in his last holy meditation. Shimmer writes, oh my god, he writes with the deepest of love:

> I bow in final acknowledgment of the healing of the broken *Hallelujah* . . .

We're going to be playing "Hallelujah," our weekly hymn and a testament to the holy and broken *Hallelujah.*

Writes Shimmer: *Its is a testament to the evolutionary human heart rooted in and as acceptance of service to the one heart shared here.*

We're bowing to you Shimmer. We're loving you outrageously as you have loved us all year in Evolutionary Church, and all year in the planetary awakening accelerator.

I read it one more time with the deepest of love, says Shimmer,

I bow in a final acknowledgment of the healing of the broken *Hallelujah* as a testament to the evolutionary human heart rooted in and as acceptance of service to the one heart shared here.

Shimmer says right. He says this with the deepest of love.

So, the question is my friends, it's only one question we ever get to ask in this world: How deep is your love?

So, Evolutionary Church, let's see it *how deep is your love* honoring Shimmer—celebration of life and death—*How deep is your love?*

Come closer, open up my eyes, tell me who I am, let me in on all your secrets, no inhibition, no sin, how deep is your love?

Is it like the ocean? What devotion? Are you *how deep is your love*? I never know how deep is your love. *Pull me closer* is *tell me how deep is your love.*

It's the only question that we ever ask, it's the only question that matters: *How deep is your love?*

Let me be your air.
Let me roam your body freely, right?

No inhibition, no fear, beyond shame. Ordinary love is not like *nirvana*. Ordinary love is a strategy of the ego.

Outrageous Love is *nirvana* itself. Hit me harder again. Open up my eyes and tell me who I am because love is a Unique Self perception.

When I love you, I see that you are a unique expression of *Homo amor universalis.* Let me in on all your secrets. No inhibition, no sin, because I realize every mistake was in the right direction, and I need only to amend and shift my intention. I am clear and I am clean. How deep is your love?

Barbara spoke to us of continuity of consciousness. We're not at the end. We are not before a tragedy. Death is both tragic and completely post-tragic.

Barbara and I talked before this call. Death is both tragic and a celebration at the same time. Death is celebration when Shimmer models for us how to live and how to die. **And how to live and how to die is to live fully, outrageously, loving every moment open and then understanding that not every moment is going to get left open.**

It's not always perfect, and we hold the imperfection; we delight in the imperfection. And we realize that we're not alone. We realize that we're held; that Reality intended Shimmer-ness.

Reality intended Shimmer's birth and Marc's birth because every one of us is going to wake up one morning on a day that will be our last.

Every single one of us in the not-too-distant future, whether it's decades or months or years, every one of us is going to wake up on a morning which we're going to breathe our last breath—every single one of us, no exceptions.

And we're going to face that place where all of the public posturing doesn't matter; all of the accumulation of blockers of pain won't matter; all the ways we covered up the hole won't matter.

One thing is going to matter:

- How deep is your love?
- How much did I love?
- How much did I love with outrageous integrity?
- How much did I put my life on the line for that which matters?
- How much did I align with truth?
- How much did I speak truth to power?

. . . and we might think that our broad public declarations are what is going to count. That's not what's going to count. I promise you, I swear to you on my life, that's not what counts.

It's the private decisions we make of integrity, it's the places we decide to stand where no one can call us out for not standing; everyone's going to tell us we shouldn't be doing it, but we know that in that moment we are vocationally aroused as *Homo amor* and we want to be in that moment lived as love. And in that moment, we're asked one question by Cosmos: *How deep is your love?*

That's what Shimmer's telling us.

There's one question to ask: *How deep is your love?*

Are you like Rhoda and Shimmer who've spent the last months coming together? Do you think they had an easy ride? Do you think they didn't have holy and broken *Hallelujahs*? Do you think their love story was all just strewn rose petals? Well, it wasn't. It was deep and difficult, hard and painful—full of closings and openings, contractions and clenches. But they knew how to answer the question: *How deep is your love?*

They said it's so deep, it's so gorgeous, that they were able to take all of their holy and broken *Hallelujahs* and know that they were always held, that they were always following, that we are always following in the arms of the Beloved.

We are so inspired by Rhoda and Shimmer. Rhoda and Shimmer are going to be with us all through church. They're going to be with us next week. Rhoda will be with us in person, and Shimmer will be with us from the other world. I promise you.

But we're going to actually pray this week like we do every week.

We're going to do our weekly hymn, "Hallelujah," and then we're going to affirm the dignity of our personal need, and we're going to ask for everything, but inspired by Shimmer. The gift we're giving Shimmer is the last wild inspiration and impact he's having on the world.

Your impact on the world is what raises your soul on the next journey.

The more we let ourselves be impacted by Shimmer in this church, the more we're giving jet propulsion, Outrageous Love fuel to his transition. That's the Physics of the universe.

- I open my closure.
- I let Shimmer impact me.
- I pray for what I've never prayed, dream what I've never dreamed.
- I am being outrageous like I've never been outrageous.

We're going to do the *Holy and Broken Hallelujah* hymn, then we're going to pray and we're going to ask for everything. **Prayer affirms the dignity of personal need. We turn, not to god the cosmic vending machine, we turn to God who is the infinite depth of love, who is the Infinity of Intimacy.**

See, my friends, the answer to the question of *how deep is your love* is God.

How deep is your love, God? How deep is your love, Barbara? How deep is your love, Marc? How deep is your love?

We are unique expressions of that, so let's pray.

Let's bring our holy and our broken *Hallelujah*, right, the celebration of everything, and we'll take it inside.

"Hallelujah," Leonard Cohen [See Appendix]

. . .

Maybe I've been here before.
I know this room, I've walked this floor.
I used to live alone before I knew you.
I've seen your flag on the marble arch.
I've heard a mortal heart and she's got a fixed new heart.
This is cold and it is unbroken.
Hallelujah, Hallelujah, Hallelujah, Hallelujah.
Maybe there's a God above
And all I ever learned from love
Was how to shoot at someone who I threw ya

It's not a cry you hear at night
It's not somebody who's seen the light
It's a cold and it's a broken Hallelujah

Thank you, thank you. Shimmer, feeling into the depth of your love. And feeling that love is the impulse of God, loving.

As God is loving as you, through you, on you, as you go onward. And Shimmer, I am somehow through you today, taking the perspective of God as us, and specifically, Shimmer, God as you.

It makes me cry to think of God, and the perspective of God, creating this entire universe with all the beings. It has taken the intention of God.

Let's feel it inside Shimmer and then feel it inside ourselves; and feel it inside the world for me, the intention of God is to create godlings. The intention of Creator is to create co-creators.

Now, if God were just intending to create robots in the image of God, none of this would have happened. But in order for Creator to create co-creators, he's had to put freedom in the system.

God had to put freedom in the system to create beings able to be strong enough to get through the process of creating a new world.

God is not just interested in creating individual aspects of co-creator. God is creating this earth as one of billions and billions of planetary systems. This earth is to be an expression of the co-creator intention of the Universe.

This church is a church of the expression of the co-creative intention of the universe itself, through every single one of us, constantly saying and declare our greatness.

Shimmer, we're declaring your greatness, for it is an expression of your gift of God to the Earth. It is an expression of God to give you post-birth, post-life, post-universal life, as you go.

I have asked myself, what is God's intention for post-universal life? What I received was: *God's intention is that your intention for life everlasting, however you choose to see it, is the next stage of freedom.*

Now, I don't know what you all think about that—that God is putting the choice at the time of dying into this sequence of life to *be intending* what comes next. Let's take this moment, Shimmer, with you and everybody in this church to join with whatever that intention is—in you.

And with you, Shimmer, fusing your love into every one of us, giving us your courage of your journey and Rhoda's courage that we may incarnate the incredible beauty of the two of you in this exact moment.

We're giving this to each other and we're taking the perspective of God's joy in this moment, because what God's saying is *it took a long time to get to people like you.*

> It really, really took a long time to get to an Evolutionary Church, says God, I never really wanted to be preserved in the old churches. I didn't. I wanted to give to every dwelling place of God the experience of the freedom of Evolutionary Love, the freedom of life everlasting, the freedom of healing the entire planet from its illusion of separation.
>
> I wanted a church to do this, and I wanted a celebration of Shimmer going into the light beyond this light to be done in this church and to be experiencing with you the power of God.

As co-creator of life on this Earth, God is co-creating the life beyond this Earth. There's no way it would stop here. No way.

So, Shimmer, my darling, my friend, I would like us just to take a moment of deep collective impulse of evolution that we are fusing inside you so that we're with you the whole way and you're opening the way for us as well as for yourself. We're with you, Shimmer.

ALL THE GATES ARE OPEN

Amen. Amen, my friends. Can you feel that?

Let's hold the silence. You can feel in this moment that all the gates are open. Can you feel that? All the gates are open. Shimmer is before his journey. Many others in the world are before their journey in this moment.

But we in our space, in our particularity, here, right now, we feel the gates open, and when you feel all the gates open, when we're in this space-in-between, it's a time of breaking.

It's a breaking of vessels. We're breaking the old structure. We're breaking our hearts. It's a time of broken vessels and broken hearts and broken structures. But in this moment, they're not breaking down. They're breaking open.

At this moment of breaking open, *bring it back to your life* and ask, *How deep is your love? And how deep is your love means where can I love more?*

Where can I ask permission and be precise in relationship in a way that exceeds, that deepens?

Where can I love more and be more and give more? Where can I be more vulnerable?

Am I willing to be in my armor-less vulnerability? Am I willing to choose to miss you? Am I willing to choose to love you?

You see, it's in those hidden moments, in those hidden moments between us, when we sit in the hole, when we don't clench and we don't close, when we feel the rage and the anger and the alienation rising, then we rest and we just stay in the whole and we say, *How deep is your love?*

We ask new words. We say, *hey, do I have permission to love you this way? Would you love me that way?* It's in the armor-less vulnerability of two human beings who are coming together in a unique Eros. A unique God is Eros.

God is union as Rhoda and Shimmer are union, as whole mates are union. We come together as Evolutionary Love partners, and we look into each other's eyes and we say, *I'm not playing a power game—How deep is your love?*

And we say to ourselves, *how deep is my love?*

That's what we're asking. Anyone who's willing to ask that question, that's the only question we ever ask: **How deep is my love?**

Find what is there that *I can do in this moment* that answers that question.

I want to invite everyone, inspired, breathed into, as Shimmer draws his last breaths by choice, as he works through the cancer in this transition. As his last breaths are drawn, they're drawn into us and we ask, **How deep is my love?**

Everyone has to answer that question individually.

Mosa made a beautiful, gorgeous video and we're going to have Mosa playing to Shimmer as we answer that question.

Then when we come back, I'm just going to ask people: *Do you have a yes to that? Is there something new that you have a yes to*, which is saying, *I'm going to step up in a way that I never have.*

How deep is my love?

We have a question. Our question is, *how deep is your love?* We ask each other this question every day, we go back and forth. We say, *how deep is your love? How much am I willing to stand?*

My friends, my friends, this is our day. It happens to be Shimmer today. Shimmer is infinite gorgeousness.

Then it's going to be Barbara, or it'll be Marc first. And it's going to be Oriana and Priscilla and Diana and Chahat, right, and Lirazi. Every one of us is going to come to this moment.

The only source of the fear of death is a life unlived. The only fear of death is if there's a piece of life unlived. And any piece of life unlived leaves in its wake a piece of fear.

A piece of life unlived, sometimes it's public. Sometimes it's a book. Sometimes it's huge and planetary. My inclination, my love—I love individuals.

But actually, the life unlived is in exchange. Was I not present? Did I not love deeply enough? And most importantly, where's the place that I'm clenched, that I haven't been able to give up? I've been able to do everything but that.

So, if we want to give Shimmer a gift this morning, and we do, and if we want to give Rhoda a gift this morning, and we do, I want to invite us to the following question:

Am I willing to say, *yes, my love is deeper than it was before.*

Yes, my love is deeper than it was before.

I'm willing to do something that I've never been willing to do before, so I am willing, *yes.*

Shimmer, *yes*. We're saying *yes* to Shimmer. Shimmer, *yes*, you've inspired me. My love is deeper than it was before.

Something has happened . . . wonder. We're the radical wonder of the moment. The phenomenology of wonder breaks the moment open, and our brain stops being in its repetition pattern, and we're blown away. This is an original moment.

Yes, Beloved, my love is deeper than it was before. That's the *Yes*.

That's the *Yes* that we're saying to Shimmer, that Shimmer's asking us today. He's asking us, *how deep is your love?* He's asking us, *are we willing to love in a way that we've never loved before?*

So I want to ask you this, but not as *I. Are you willing to love in a way that you've never loved before?* **Are you willing to love in a way that you have never loved before?** That's the question. *Are you willing to love?*

Let the *yes* explode. The holy *yes* of the Big Bang is happening right now. **Yes, I am willing to love in a way that I have never been loved before.**

If you think that we should be low key about this, you think this is low key, oh my god, *are you really, for real?*

It's so gentle—it's so quivering tenderness and such radical audacity. Yes and yes and yes. That is what Evolutionary Church is—it's celebration. It's *Homo amor universalis*. As Barbara said, *it's continuity of consciousness.* We are the planetary voice for *Homo amor universalis*. How deep is your love?

Deepest love, the end and silence of presence.

CHAPTER EIGHT

LOVE IS IN THE DETAILS — RECLAIMING THE POWER OF WORDS AND WONDER

Episode 78 — April 14, 2018

LOVE IS IN THE DETAILS

This code is of radical importance both in our personal lives and in our social lives. Read with what we call *radical amazement* because it goes so deep, and it's so simple, and it truly makes all the difference.

Here is the Evolutionary Love Code:

> *Homo amor universalis* has unique Outrageous Acts of Love to commit. Those acts of love are those that we can get away with not doing.

> They may be smiling when we want to withhold. It's changing our tone of voice, it's sending a text with an overflowing heart, it's taking a stand when we can get away with not taking a stand.

> Genuine, Outrageous Acts of Love are the fabric of *Homo amor universalis*.

> For true Outrageous Acts of Love, we can always explain to ourselves why we don't have to do it. Outrageous Acts of Love are when we give

ourselves outrageously—beyond our traumas, our rackets, our issues, and our patterns.

What moves us to commit Outrageous Acts of Love is evolution herself, Goddess Herself, She.

One of the most fascinating things about this code is the question of who is in charge of whether we speak with love or not. Where does that decision—*decidere* meaning "to cut off in Latin—where does that decision get made?

Can you experience a time when somebody has been hurtful to you, and you want to cut off from them because you've been hurt, and you're reacting and responding to that hurt? It can be so subtle, such as they might have not smiled at you one day. They might not have said hello to you. They might not have responded to an email and you felt hurt, and so then you refuse to respond to theirs. These are tiny little things, but you could make the choice as an Outrageous Evolutionary Lover to notice and feel every one of those moments and still say *yes* to love.

The accumulation of these decisions will greatly impact everybody's life: It's changing our tone of voice, it's sending a text with an overflowing heart, it's taking a stand when we can get away with not taking a stand.

What's so beautiful about this is that all the love is in the details, and the details compose the whole, minute by minute and second by second. So, get in touch right now with someplace where you have not smiled back or you have not responded because you were slightly hurt. Can you think of something like that?

Now, imagine yourself in this situation, but responding with love—genuine Outrageous Love, genuine Outrageous Evolutionary Acts of Love are the fabric of *Homo amor universalis*. **This new species that we are co-creating is being created by our minute-by-minute decisions**.

Think of every cell in your body as unique, and yet, if it goes astray uniquely—if it does not stay with the process of the whole system—it causes cancer, just a cell. If I, as an individual, don't respond lovingly to somebody who possibly ignored me or hurt me, I am a cancerous cell in the social body. I am creating a society that is not *Homo amor universalis.* **In Outrageous Acts of Love we give ourselves outrageously, wholly and completely, with no defense system or protection that makes sure we're as good as, or better than someone else.** These are tiny, little things that make all the difference.

- *Beyond our traumas*, our hurts, or our rackets. Well, my racket is God. I'm an evolutionary agent of the highest order and, therefore, I should be appreciated.
- *Beyond our issues and our patterns.* If you could think for the moment of your issues and your patterns, it is what might make you reactive rather than proactive in love.

What moves us to commit Outrageous Acts of Love is evolution Herself, Goddess Herself, She. Get in touch with *She* inside yourself. The impulse of evolution as you, uniquely as you, saying *Yes*, to love in the details.

REWEAVING GOD AND RECLAIMING CELEBRATION

The CosmoErotic Universe in person is *Homo amor universalis.* We were studying together last week, and you know that this sentence just kind of emerged, so clearly: ***Homo amor universalis* is the CosmoErotic Universe in person, and it is all personal.** The globalists are personal, and what happens in Syria is personal, but we can't start there, because if we start there, we are bypassing the actual invitation of our lives. None of us gets to decide today, yet, what happens in Syria the next day, although we should and can be radical activists to influence Syria.

What each of us can do right now is give up being right and become *Homo amor universalis* in the details, in the thickness of our lives, with the people that we take for granted.

Evolutionary Church, in the beginning and the end, is a celebration. Now, that seems like an easy thing to say, but I want to put a distinction in place here which is core to the church. We're losing the power of celebration. Instead of celebrating, we typically want to sit back and be amused or entertained. We have an entertainment industry and entertainment, in some deep sense, has replaced celebration. Let's reclaim celebration:

- *Celebration is an active state*, Abraham Joshua Heschel would write.
- The mystics talked about celebration as an act of reverence.
- Celebration is an act of devotion.
- Celebration is an act of radical amazement.

To be entertained is a passive state. It's to receive pleasure afforded by an amusing actor or spectacle. But celebration, write the erotic mystics, is a confrontation.

In celebration, we give attention to the transcendent meaning of our actions.

So, let's reweave celebration into our church. In Evolutionary Church we're reweaving the source code of Reality itself. We are in this da Vinci moment and we're saying, *Let's reweave what we mean by God*. We worry so much about the separation of church and state. Maybe we should worry about the separation of church and God. You can go to church and never meet God. God's not a nice guy. God's not your aunt. God's not your uncle. God is an earthquake! The realization of God is a radical, shimmering, earthquake. When you say for one moment *I know God*, everything changes. The way you speak, the way you move, the way you gesture. **God is the very gesture of Cosmos, and we pray and we love from that place.**

Homo amor universalis is always seeking to know God. Not the god you don't believe in. That's been our principle in Evolutionary Church: *the god you don't believe in doesn't exist*. Not prayer to a Santa Claus god, but to the God who is the earthquake of Evolutionary Love, radically animating with dazzling exponentially, beyond super-computer, gorgeous brilliance, in each one of our bodies right now.

WORDS ARE THE VESSELS OF SPIRIT

Let's turn inside. Let's just go into our body for one second and feel millions of miles of nerve cable in our body right now, operating with such synchronicity, with such beauty, with such incandescent, glowing, mathematical brilliance. It is so obviously uniquely designed for each one of us, and it is happening right now.

Then, there's this way that we can talk to each other. There's a way to have thought and will that emerges out of us. We can speak to each other and interact in a way that creates new gnosis. We are new and unique, and it is all so shocking.

This is the ground of the Evolutionary Church. In Evolutionary Church, we believe in words. A memetic structure is a way we form words. One of the principles that we are talking about is that every human being is a unique configuration of intimacy. So, when we come together and bring words together in a certain way, we create a new organism. That is called a new meme.

We bring together words to create a new meme, a new memetic structure that evolves the source code. We use words today as tools, *Homo habilis*. These become tools to accomplish low functions. But words are cathedrals of Spirit.

> *Words are the vessels of Spirit, and the vessels today are broken.*

We cannot evolve the source code unless we reclaim a reverence—our wonder—for words. Every word between us matters. The way we speak to each other matters. Words are *Abra Kadabra*, in Aramaic, which means: *I speak. I create*. Words are magic; we evolve the source code through words. So let's look at prayer.

What is prayer? What do we mean by prayer? How does prayer work? Prayer is a revolutionary act. When Abraham Joshua Heschel went with Martin Luther King to march on Selma, he said, *I'm praying with my feet.*

- Prayer is revolution. Prayer is when I turn to the Infinity of Intimacy that knows my name, that manifested, and that is close to, part of, connected to, and lives as my unique configuration of intimacy.
- Prayer says that the need of every individual is my need, and the pathos of every individual is my pathos.
- Prayer says that God knows my name, knows my desperation, knows my roughness, knows my rapture, knows my gorgeousness, and knows my beauty.
- Prayer says that God needs me. God needs me to pray, because in prayer, we affirm the dignity of personal need.

In prayer, we say no one is left out of the circle. In prayer, we say that as long as you speak, God listens. In prayer, we say God's both within me and holding me in every moment, and every place I fall, I fall into Her hands. That's true of every human being on the planet. If someone, somehow is not held, I am not held, and if someone's gorgeous uniqueness is not recognized, then I am not recognized.

I'm going to tell you a little secret about how I (Marc) get through suffering. I meditate and I chant, and that's all true. I do some meditation, but primarily, I engage in a certain kind of reflective chant, which is the core of my practice. Often, even chanting can't quite get me home.

Then I do a simple meditation to move me out of an experience sometimes—often a daily experience—of intense suffering. I do what I call a narcissist meditation. It is a great meditation. I experience whatever suffering I might be experiencing and then I ask myself:

> Okay, well, before this or that caused me to experience that suffering, did I function and was I happy and delighted in the world? Well, the answer is yes, I was totally happy and delighted.

Then I say to myself:

> One second I was happy and delighted, but there was the
> genocide in Rwanda going on, and there was the war in Bosnia
> going on, and there was the civil war in Syria going on. How
> could I have been happy and delighted if all that stuff was going
> on? Oh, because that thing hadn't happened to you. Oh, I see.
> So the only way your actual mood is affected is if it affects you,
> but, the rest of the world doesn't matter. Well then, you must be
> a narcissist.

Now, the idea of being a narcissist is so shocking and so horrific, that it
breaks my heart. Then my heart just breaks open for the suffering of the
world and then whatever suffering I have is washed away, and held in that
sea of suffering.

When I stay in that suffering, and then feel God in that suffering, I feel She
is there with me. Then the suffering of everyone—mine and everyone's—
turns to sweetness because I know that every place we have been, we
needed to be.

In some sense, with all of its tragedy and suffering, Reality is intended by
the Divine to grow us, to breathe us, to love us madly, and to invite us into
partnership, even as we stand on the edge of the abyss and the edge of
mystery.

That's what prayer is: we bring it all to God. We bring our holy and our
broken *Hallelujah*. We bring every piece of our lives. In Evolutionary
Church we stand together for evolving the source code.

A COSMOEROTIC STORY EQUAL TO THE STORY OF CHRIST

I (Barbara) have had an experience of the entire story of creation as personal,
resulting in exactly this moment where I can choose to love personally.

It happened one day when I was irritated after reading the story of Christ in the Bible and I said to the universe, **Okay, that story was great and it reached all humanity. But what story could humanity tell now equal to the story of the birth of Christ?** I looked up at the universe and I asked. Jesus said, *ask and it is given, knock and the door shall open.* This applies to all of our prayers. I became evolution. I remember exactly the experience of being at the Big Bang, the explosion, and feeling the allurement of all particles to each other.

Then I was able to allow the process to move in me, which is alive in every one of us. **Every one of us is a living, breathing, example of 13.8 billion years of genius, as exactly who we uniquely are.** So, when we are thinking of the details of our lives and the exact moment that we're in, we place that within the huge impulse, direction, and genius of evolution. What that does is deeply affect your unique prayer, because you have placed the prayer in the context of this greatness.

So, I experienced the hydrogen. Brian Swimme said that *the universe could have been satisfied with hydrogen.* Well, obviously, it wasn't. Why wasn't it satisfied with hydrogen, any more than it is satisfied with us? Because there is something deeper going on here that is us in action, in this Evolutionary Church. So, as I went up I could feel every single cell in my body coming into form, into ever more complex form, until I got to the present moment as evolution itself. I felt as a reality within me the allurement of every particle to every other particle. In other words, I experienced the internalization of the allurement process of evolution itself.

I remembered that as a very little girl I had heard about somebody torturing somebody else. I remember this very deep feeling of, well, this is not normal. That was at six years old, and yet, what did I know about *normal*? I just knew, intrinsically, that it was not normal to be able to torture somebody else. It felt to me as though something had gone wrong with evolution itself. I didn't even have the concept of evolution, but that something went wrong when somebody could behave that way to somebody else.

I kept asking myself the question, *What went wrong?* I was a very happy child. I lived a privileged life. I was with people who loved and cared for me. I walked to school every day in New York City and had a great time. Then, the United States dropped the atomic bombs on Japan, and this question of what went wrong then rose to be the question of my life. **What went wrong that we could drop a bomb on thousands of people and burn them alive?**

What went wrong? My family thought it was really good that we did this because we won the war. And then this realization came, and I think this is why I'm in the Evolutionary Church today. I spoke to God and told him:

This is wrong, and the misuse of power.

This power is not going to stop just with nuclear but will get greater and greater. Indeed it hasn't, it has gone all the way up to biotech, and nanotech, and quantum computing, and so on, artificial intelligence.

If you created all of our intelligence which could understand this degree of how nature works, $e=mc^2$, and then make a bomb, then what is your process now, of awakening us to the right use of power?

What can we learn from you, God, that could activate in us your triumph of a species capable of loving God with all this power, which would mean co-creating a new world? It would be a new Earth, a new heaven, and a new everything.

I kept right on with this question about *what went wrong?* and discovered, of course, mainly through the Jesuit, Teilhard de Chardin, that God had put a purpose in evolution for greater consciousness, more freedom, and more complex order, and that we were about to hit a new threshold, which he called the *Ultra-Human*, where the noosphere, getting its collective eyes, would be overwhelmed consciously within the innate process of love itself. I began to think that maybe that is the exact moment we are in now. *Homo amor universalis* **is a species filled with love with the powers of the universal process of creation, spiritually, socially, and technologically.**

Homo amor universalis is the expression, in person, of the CosmoErotic Universe. Is it possible that we are the generation coming up out of *Homo sapiens*, who has been the greatest killer that the world has ever known, and also the greatest lover? The most brilliant, but most separated from one another?

Is it possible that what's happening right now is evolution by human choice, not by chance— what we call Conscious Evolution—is now going to be made by members of the new species Homo amor universalis, who choose to participate in the CosmoErotic Universe?

Could our deepest purpose be to choose to align with Evolutionary Love within ourselves so profoundly that it has taken 13.8 billion years for She to create this opportunity? It has taken this long for the opportunity for a shift of Evolutionary Love, *en masse* on this planet, as the entire species faces devolution, through misuse of our powers, or evolution, through the proper use of our powers? In other words, this is the exact moment in the history of Planet Earth, where this choice is being offered, and it is being offered in the details of this church.

The Church of Evolutionary Love is being created by those choosing to enter the new species, to create the next stage of evolution, both personally in small ways and collectively as it results in the new humanity.

HOMO AMOR UNIVERSALIS IS AWESTRUCK

Let's be awestruck by the power, the beauty, and the truth of us being here in this moment. I want to invite us to this sense of wonder because that is what *Homo amor universalis* feels as the CosmoErotic Universe in person. Wonder comes from the details. Let's face it: we're all a little bit like miniature addicts: we don't let ourselves be moved; we're not radically amazed. **Being addicted means that I'm not in awe of the beauty of my Beloved, my partner, my friend, or my co-creator.**

I start losing the ability to have my heart broken open in love. Something closes and freezes in my heart, and it's almost always because of something at a very young, or some very early hurt in this life or possibly in a previous life. Something shatters in my heart. Something closes and I don't quite know how to open it again. What happens then is I stop being in the original moment.

My (Marc) teacher, Leiner would always ask one question. I wrote about a thousand pages on this in a book called Radical *Kabbalah*, about Leiner. Leiner asked one question: *Can you ever have an original moment? Can you ever be original, or is every moment basically a repetition?* Brain science teaches us that our brain is an entrainment machine that seeks to make sure that we stay safe and soothe our early trauma and anxiety.

So, whenever we are confronted with a situation, the brain immediately brings up all the old situations that are in any way parallel to that situation and then collates the best response that will soothe us and keep us safe. What that means, as neuroscientist Antonio Damasio points out, is that the brain is a repetition machine; I'm actually never here. I'm never in Evolutionary Church. Once I've gone to a couple of Evolutionary Churches, I'm literally not here anymore. I may be responding positively, indifferently, or even in my joy, but my joy is regurgitated joy; it's the old response.

How do I get out of the old response and into the moment? The name of God is the *Yud* in Hebrew: the eternal, eternity, gorgeousness, that lives in the *Hey Vav Hey*, which is the present. It is the Eternity. It is the *now-ing*. Let's introduce an Evolutionary Church practice, now-ing. Now-ing means I am living the name of God, right here, right now. **I can live in the now only if I am willing to break my heart open again and again.**

The only way to live in the now is to be willing to break your heart open again and again.

And when you break your heart open, you're filled with joy; and sometimes that joy involves pain, and sometimes involves hurting more than we want to hurt.

To be a *Homo amor universalis,* to be the CosmoErotic Universe in person, means I break my heart open every day.

How do I do that? How do we get out of the repetition? We get out of the repetition through radical amazement. Are we willing to be radically blown away by each other? Am I willing to let you blow me away? Am I willing to listen to you and be blown away? Am I willing to be blown away by every word, every gesture? We are struck. We are blown away by each other. We are radically amazed by each other.

The erotic mystics say that our goal should be to live in radical amazement. To get up in the morning and look at the world in a way that nothing is a given. I take nothing for granted. Everything is phenomenal. To be a phenomenologist is that everything's phenomenal, but not in a sugar-coated New Age kind of way. I am blown away by the detailed wonder. Everything is so gorgeous. **To be spiritual is to be radically amazed.** *Awe* is a beautiful word:

- Awe is the intuition of the gorgeous beauty and dignity in all things.
- Awe is a realization that things are not only what they are, but everything stands for something, everything alludes to something supreme.
- Awe, the erotic mystics write, is a sense of transcendence.
- Awe is a sense that everything is a reference to the mystery beyond all things.

- Awe enables us to perceive the glimmerings of the Divine everywhere.

To be intimate is to know that everything in the world is an intimation of the ultimate mystery. To sense the ultimate in the common and the simple. To feel the rush of gorgeous, Outrageous Love in every detail. Heschel wrote, *What we cannot comprehend by analysis, we become aware of through awe.*

The opposite of good is not evil; the opposite of good is indifference.

Our prayer is to open our eyes in wonder. Break my heart open in wonder. Break my heart, not in a way that hurts, but just break my heart open in wonder. Break my heart open and just feel it. That is our prayer.

Our prayer is, *I am Homo amor universalis, and let wonder speak to me, and let me be awestruck.* **That is our deepest prayer, to break my heart open in wonder, so I can be radically amazed by you, so I can take nothing for granted, so I can be so radically filled with gratitude that I become an activist.** My narcissism does not leave me wondering about the depth of my own personal experience, which is gorgeous; but I ride my pain and I ride my joy into God's pain and God's joy.

Break my heart open with wonder. Wow, break my heart open. My friends, it's so easy to forget.

CHAPTER NINE

CLOSING THE GAP BETWEEN OUR ABILITY TO FEEL AND TO HEAL

Episode 79 — April 21, 2018

OUTRAGEOUS LOVE MOVES THROUGH US

Hello everyone, welcome to Evolutionary Church.

Let's blow the moment open now and allow the radical power of desire, of evolutionary desire, of the impulse of creation to come through us as I read this code for today.

We close our hearts in the gap between our ability to feel the pain, and we open our hearts by responding to the capacity to heal the pain. When we think of the pain that is going around us from personal, all the way to planetary, we close our hearts often because we can't feel it all. *It's too much.* Now, let's open them completely with the capacity to heal. But one of the problems of allowing it all in is you can't heal it all. So, we feel inadequate and close the door.

Here's the solution.

We do not (and we realize we do not) need to heal the whole. Rather, we each have unique Outrageous Acts of

Love that are the unique expression of our own Unique Self. What happens to you when you say *yes:*

- to express that uniqueness of your being,
- that only you can do,
- toward a pain or a sorrow or a hurt . . .

. . . you're beginning to heal it through expressing uniqueness.

What's happening to you? How do you feel when you commit an act of Outrageous Love that you and you alone can commit?

That's really, really the question.

By doing that you blow yourself open and you allow the flow of Outrageous Love to go through you as you bring it outward toward someone that you are saying, *yes*, I can heal you.

If you don't open the door to the Outrageous Love that can heal somebody else, it can't heal you either. It stays within.

And so those alone, we have the capacity to do—even though there are 20 good reasons, financial, familial, psychological, rational not to take them and not to do them.

Those unique outrageous acts are the path and purpose of our incarnation.

Let's just take a moment before we close to go within and discover the most outrageous act of love that you are called to do to meet a specific need in someone else, whether personal, social or planetary or even within yourself and feel yourself giving it the whole way and what happens, it takes you the whole way because once you turn on the outrageous act of love, it has no limits.

It is outrageous. It is the Evolutionary Love that moves the entire process of creation moving through you.

OUR COMMITMENT IS TO TELL A NEW STORY

It is such a delight. Let's just feel the delight, and let's just pause for a second.

Barbara, Beloved, you have set us in our resonant field and we are in this new code, we are delighted. Feel the delight right now. I just feel it.

I want to just do a kind of personal check-in just for one second to share something that's happening in this moment as we feel the delight. Then I want to say something about the beautiful code to open up into prayer and we're going to open all the gates together.

We're trying to evolve the source code. That's our commitment. Our commitment is to tell a new story, you know, we have different languages for it to awaken the new humanity to become the new human, to evolve the source code of consciousness and culture.

This Evolutionary Church is not a desktop application.

This is a source code move. This is not desktop. We are in the source code and we are holding that radical audacity and that radical humility.

Humility means we're transparent to the Evolutionary Love that moves through us.

Audacity is we're responsible to what that means, that we are the ones that are in this moment in history, bringing together the mimetic codes to tell the new story—the story of identity, the narrative of power, the narrative of meaning, the new Universe Story, the narrative of Eros, the narrative of entrepreneurship, medicine, education.

We're bringing together a source of mimetic codes, like da Vinci did in Florence and Venice that are ushering in, bringing in, calling in, demanding that we step up as the new humans and become the new humanity.

Now, I have for the last several years, you know—in this kind depth of this Eros—I've been trying to work something out, which is: I came from a particular lineage, and my affiliation in the world today, my community, my association is around the world. It's in this vision of what I like to call world spirituality.

We started *the center* as the Center for World Spirituality, and we changed it to the Center for Wisdom.

Barbara's gorgeous location is in Conscious Evolution. We're locating, we're joining memes, we're joining genius in this cosmocentric, world-centric, you know, mood, **but to articulate a genuine set of obligations, a genuine set of practices—a genuine set of principles and insights, the core mimetic structures**. But what happens about what we left behind? What happens to lineages? In a world spirituality, what happens to yesterday?

To be in integrity with today, we have to be in integrity with yesterday.

I want to put that in our space as we move into prayer.

Whenever we're involved in development (meaning we're developing) we are evolving, we always have to transcend and include the level that came before.

The mistake, for example, of Modernity was it rejected *all of the truths* of the great traditions and then created a new modern vision, which is beautiful, but didn't take with it the deepest intuitions of that spirit that were shared by all the great traditions.

Instead, it correctly critiqued the shadows of the great traditions, but didn't take the best of the great traditions with it.

And postmodernity critiqued Modernity. It critiqued its failure to include LGBT, and critiqued its hidden racism, and critiqued its gender bias, but it failed to take with us the best intuitions from Modernity, which are wildly important.

So, for me personally…

- As I'm moving in life
- As I'm with Barbara
- As I'm with our entire gang at the Foundation for Conscious Evolution, at the Center for Integral Wisdom, all of us together,

. . . we're trying to unfold this new memetic field. **We're trying to tell the new story—da Vinci-like, as it were.**

I asked myself, and I've meditated on this for the last couple years, *what am I missing? What do I need to do to be in integrity?* And I realized what I need to do was, I need to reclaim my formal relationship to the law of the lineage in which I was born.

Now I've never abandoned that relationship. I practiced the law of my lineage to some large extent, but the parts of it that got hard, I let go. For example, not driving on the Sabbath, which is the formal law—I let go, because I'm not in a community that has any practitioners of this lineage, so it forced me to basically have everybody pick me up.

I kind of became, in an inappropriate way, the narcissistic center of attention—because I'm not in a community that in any way follows any of these laws, there was no way for me to keep them without it just not working. It's a communal practice. So, I let the practice go. I did the private practices, and I let lots of the law go as I moved beyond it.

Then I realized that I was out of integrity with the lineage masters—that in order for the Evolutionary Church to rise, Barbara needs to do what she needs to do in her world, and I need to do what I need to do, and everyone needs to do in their world. **What do we need to do to make this rise?**

I realized I need to be in full integrity with the full power of the law that I committed to 40 years ago; not publicly, it's not going to change my public position, but I realized...

- Even though it's inconvenient
- Even though there's no one in my world who practices it in any way, and
- Even though it's not relevant, not part of my communal affiliation in any way
- Even though it's wildly painful for me . . .

. . . nonetheless, my lineage obligation is to step into the law.

The reason I'm sharing that with you, is because it means that this week I'm not writing.

I'm kind of flying a little bit blind.

I'm different than other weeks, and I'm kind of in that place of the law in the maximum way that I'm able to do, which is a private integrity, meaning I need to transcend and include.

I want to invite each of you to ask yourself the following question: What do you need to do to transcend and include yesterday in order to have the power to unfold this new lineage of Evolutionary Church, this new lineage of world spirituality, this new lineage of CosmoErotic Humanism—in order to become a new human, *Homo amor universalis?*

There's thousands of us who have joined the church from around the world. This week there'll be hundreds and hundreds of people in church. The question is:

What do you need to do?

Let's get this down. *What do I need to transcend and include from yesterday that I've left behind, that I'm out of integrity for leaving that behind?* It might be a relationship. It might be a lineage commitment. For most people . . . *What is it that's unfinished? What's the unfinished business I have that is an obstacle, that is in the way.*

Without actually completing that, here's the paradox:

I never intend again in my life to teach as an orthodox rabbi, but I'll always be an orthodox rabbi even though it's not my practice. I'm not interested in practicing that. It's not what I do.

But:

+ If I'm not in integrity with the orthodox rabbi
+ If I've just left him behind
+ If I'm not in integrity with his commitments—the parts of them that I still radically believe but stopped doing because they were just hard, wildly inconvenient, or "didn't work"...

If I'm out of integrity, then I can't build the church, and we can't start this new lineage. We have to transcend and include in order to become the new human.

The new human has to bring with him/her the best of the great traditions, and the best of our particular commitments.

EVOLUTIONARY LOVE CODE: CLOSING THE GAP

Barbara and I have been formulating and working with this, and we've been working with it at the center and the foundation for many years. The core of it:

> The recognition that I tend to close my heart in the gap between my ability to feel and my ability to heal

That's the core of the code.

We can write it in our hearts. I feel the pain of the whole world. Why? Because I actually know about the pain of the whole world—I've got CNN coming at me.

Barbara and I were talking the other day that Ronald Reagan saw things on CNN that his National Security Council hadn't told him. And now we have more access to information than any other generation ever did. We see more images of suffering. *A hundred years ago the only one who saw as much suffering as we do in this generation was God.*

Only God, a hundred years ago, had more access, not just this level of information, but the level of suffering in the world.

We are constantly bombarded with images of suffering, so what do we do? We close our hearts. Why do we close our hearts? Because we can't function, so what do I do?

Barbara, do you remember Biafra? Remember the Biafra-Bangladesh story? Biafra/Bangladesh splits in half. We're watching this incredible suffering, and I'm like nine years old, eight years old, and I'm watching it, and I'm just overwhelmed, and I can't move. My mother comes in, and she flips off the channel and says *don't watch.*

I remember getting a little paper cut, and my mother reacted, Oh my god, your little finger, your paper cut!—a classic Jewish mother response: *Little finger, oh my god, your paper cut, oh my god, oh my god!*

I remember thinking to myself, *I don't get it.* I mean, my little finger's going to survive, my mom just turned off Biafra/Bangladesh, this massive suffering, not supposed to deal with that—let's deal with my little paper cut. I just remember how weird it felt to me, but that's what we're trained to do. We're trained as narcissists and we turn off—we can't feel the pain of the world.

The reason we can't feel it is not because we're bad; we can't feel it because it's too much.

There's a gap between our ability to feel the pain and our ability to heal the pain, because we can't do the whole thing, we can't fix the whole thing.

Barbara already pointed to the solution: You don't have to heal the whole thing. It's not your job. It's your job to find your place. It's my job to find my place in the Unique Self Symphony, and to play my unique instrument. It addresses that unique need with my unique gift, and my unique circle of intimacy influence. **My unique gift might not even be what I like doing most. It's a unique gift that's needed in this moment.**

When Israel was formed, the best doctors went and started learning how to plant, even though they were great doctors, because the need of *that moment* was that Israel needed to learn how to turn the desert into a place with fertile crops. So, brilliant researchers in medicine—the need of that moment was plant fields—that's what they did.

Unique needs, not necessarily what my talent is, is what is uniquely needed in my circle of intimacy and influence at this moment—that only I can do uniquely like I can. That's what I do.

As Barbara said in the code, everyone's going to tell you not to do it—but no one is going to be able to call you out. There's going to be a million reasons: familial, financial, social, psychological, to avoid. And to free yourself, though everyone's going to tell you, *Oh, you don't need to.*

You're never mandated by Reality to actually play your instrument in the symphony—only you can choose to.

There's going to be a billion rationalizations (based on Barbara Fredrickson's work[10]) for not playing your instrument.

But when you play an instrument, you wake up. You're filled with joy. You're participating in a Unique Self Symphony. All of a sudden you're able to heal; you realize *that is my healing to do*, because you're able to heal. You're able to feel again.

We close the gap between our ability to heal and our ability to feel.

THE WAY IN IS THE WAY IN TO PRAYER

The first step is we first reclaim our ability to feel. We open up that which we've closed down. We go back to the deepest well of our holy and our broken *Hallelujah*. Not in a kind of therapeutic way of *let me revisit my wounds again* in order to give me a false sense of aliveness. No.

I'm willing to feel:

- My loneliness
- My holiness
- My greatness
- My pain
- All of my holy and broken *Hallelujahs*

I'm willing to know the full gorgeous dignity of my sacred autobiography. I feel it all, and from that place of feeling it all, I embrace my Unique Self.

From there I begin to offer my unique gift. From there I begin to commit my evolutionary acts of love.

---

10   Barbara L. Fredrickson, a leading figure in positive psychology, is known for her broaden-and-build theory, which explains how positive emotions expand cognition and foster resilience without requiring individuals to "step out" of normative patterns of behavior; see *Love 2.0: How Our Supreme Emotion Affects Everything We Feel, Think, Do, and Become* (New York: Hudson Street Press, 2013).

Barbara is going to talk about what it means to identify and give my unique gift, which is my unique ability to heal, and how that opens up my ability to feel.

How do we close the gap to our ability to feel and our ability to heal? We start with just feeling ourselves. We take our holy and our broken *Hallelujah*, and we offer it up on the altar to the Infinity of Intimacy, God, who is the Infinity of Intimacy, who loves our prayer, who affirms the dignity of our personal need.

> *Every time we pray, we pray for all the times we've never prayed before. And every time we cry we cry for all the times we never cried before. So, we offer our prayer.*

My teacher, my lineage master, Abraham Kook, used to say: *If You're Not Willing to Risk Your Very Life, You're Not Praying.*

To pray means you are willing to feel so deeply that you literally risk your life in prayer. I'm willing to go all the way. I'm willing to feel it all the way.

Any feeling I don't feel the whole way comes back and hijacks the steering wheel of my life. When I feel it the whole way, it opens—and I can feel my power.

And so we pray:

> *I pray for the energy and strength to offer my unique abilities to help others and myself.*
>
> *I pray for my sister.*
>
> *I pray for our prayers to blossom in love.*

I pray for the strength to open to the pain and let it love, to heal it and heal me,

I pray to open my heart to the one heart of the world.

I can only hold others pain to the extent that I can hold my own, I pray to hold others even more.

I pray for coming closer ever to Goddess through all that I do.

WE'VE ALL LEFT SOMETHING BEHIND

A theme in church this week is *what have we left behind that we need to bring with us* in order to have the integrity to actually commit our Outrageous Acts of Love—which allow us once again to heal, and once again to *feel.*

I have an awesome revelation to share as a process of doing this.

I began to understand what is really meant by Evolutionary Love. I saw it as the core of the evolutionary spiral that created, from nothing at all, everything that is, and I realized that I spent a lot of my life practice identifying myself with that core of the spiral. As I was doing this code today, I began to ask:

> *As a as a person who is an experiential expression of the entire core of the spiral—the God force—how am I going to behave now, with the current crisis of either the breakdown of civilization or the breakthrough of Homo amor universalis* (a planetary awakening in love).

I was able to call on Evolutionary Love to be its most awesome potential through me, and through every single person who would choose to do this, so that I could flow through *Homo amor universalis* uniting it into a new Field of Love. That is like an awesome challenge.

Here's how it works.

Each of us is the core of the spiral. We are animated by it in all our personal needs—all the things that we are giving and sharing—because

we are, each of us, a planetary citizen at a time of either devolution or **Conscious Evolution.**

Here's the amazing experience.

Imagine *Homo amor universalis* as a species that is made up of a set of characteristics that we all have.

One is the very highest degree of evolutionary spirituality, so I passed as *Homo amor universalis*. **My Evolutionary Love goes up through my spirituality all the way.** While you're doing your lineage, Marc, I'm doing my lineage as a universal human. I believe it's a new lineage.

The next thing I went up through—carrying the impulse of evolution—is vocation. Everyone's vocation. Take the top off of vocation, the lid, and imagine you are going the whole way with whatever it is, along with your evolutionary spirituality and along with the impulse of creation.

This code was taking me into the whole realization, of all joining genius, of vocational arousal, and supra-sex.

I began to feel a *Homo amor universalis feeling,* a shared experience of joining genius. That is an awesome love affair. If everybody who wants to be in touch with another in order to fulfill greater life purpose was doing so as a celebration of a planetary awakening in love, the awesome experience is almost beyond belief.

Then I took high tech. I am Evolutionary Love driving high tech forward. We are Evolutionary Love; high enough, strong enough, powerful enough, to take the powers of the ancient gods and turn them into love; to do absolutely the capacity of healing the whole thing, including hunger, disease, war, and misuse of resources.

I allowed this code to go through me as a pioneer of the new human who is completely infused with the entire billions of years of Evolutionary Love.

We have a species: *Homo amor universalis.* And let's end here with human individual as a member of species *Homo amor universalis.*

The individual human, *Homo amor universalis,* in person, holds all of this; and his/her ability to heal is so great that it actually does resemble the ability of God to heal, because one thing I learned in reading about "acosmic humanism" is that there's relationship between God and human *when the will is pure.*

Acosmic humanism is the human who has completely integrated the wholeness of the will of God that resides in this human. We are human incarnations of God—fully. The word cosmic is the world; acosmic means even beyond cosmos, like a history.

I made up the word acosmic humanism, but it meant knowing that I'm part of the all, **I don't merge and disappear into the one like Buddhist mysticism would say, but by knowing I am the All, I am the entire spiral awakening in me; it's all me.**

That brings you not to disappearing, not to going into the ashram, it brings you to a humanism that is acosmic humanism—a new humanity, a new human.

THE WONDERFUL IMAGE OF THE JUDAH ARCHETYPE

The Judah archetype: You have you have such an extraordinary courage, will, and willingness to go the whole way!

What I realized in reading this (and then reading Marc's new paper on divine desire and Eros) is that the Eros of evolution that goes through that spiral—is love. The core of the spiral is that.

We're going to take a quantum jump. I'm taking a quantum jump as a new human. **I am a new human who is incarnating the full spiral of evolution, aware of the powers of the new species that we have been given to infuse with love.**

I would like to give a glorious introduction to *Homo amor universalis* in person that is designed to give birth to this *Homo amor universalis* in every member of the church. Therefore, this church changes—not only us, but the entire world—in response to the crisis of our time, as we give birth to a new species.

You can feel the excitement. There's something happening at church. **We are not revisiting tired old clichés. We're creating a new language. And together we're creating a new human—a new vision.**

Acosmic humanism is about the invoking of the new humanity. It's a non-dual humanism—the invoking of the new human and the new humanity.

Of course Barbara was doing that off in her corner, and I was doing it off in my corner, and we hadn't met. Now we're bringing the means to what's so exciting, so Barbara and the cosmic humanism, and what I call the Judah archetype.

The Judah archetype is the predecessor of Unique Self, Evolutionary Unique Self, and Homo amor universalis.

Our word that we're going to try and inscribe in God's lips this week is: *I'm willing to go the whole way*—but we're not there yet. Let's see if we can find our way there. It's awesome.

There are two moves. Move one is the move of modernity that didn't take with it the integrity of the previous lineages. Modernity said, we're creating a new lineage, we're the universal human, but modernity forgot to take with it the deep realizations of the old traditions. It saw that the old traditions made mistakes: they were homophobic; they were anti-science; their ways of gathering information was messed up; they were mutually exclusive; they were fighting wars; they were elitist; they were a mess.

But modernity forgot to take with it the best of the great traditions:

- The realization of Spirit
- That Spirit is real
- Spirit lives on the inside
- The world is more than material
- Interiors are real
- Love, loyalty, and desire—these are all real they're not just fabricated

Life is not just about what Darwin called survival. Life is about growth and transformation. We want to align with the interior consciousness.

REALITY IS ALIVE AND IT'S CONSCIOUS

The hills are alive the sound of music; the hills are alive and Reality is alive; Reality is conscious. It's not just material. Modernity missed that.

So, modernity kind of went and said *let's talk about human humanism.* But humanism was against divine-ism. You get it: the human being is the center? That was Michaelangelo's *new image* in the Sistine Chapel and really the center of everything is the human being; God is on the side—either God is erased or God is an occasional person that you invite to decorate.

Whoa! That's completely different than the great traditions. Even the Eastern tradition said forget about human being, even being supposed to absorb himself as part of the One; get rid of your personality that is in the way; get rid of all that stuff that's in the way; merge with the one— the famous Zen hot dog joke, *make me one with everything.* It's one with everything.

It's what I said in this in this two-volume work that I did.[11] It's this deep uncovering of this understanding of what we call acosmic or nondual

---

11   Marc Gafni, *Radical Kabbalah: The Early Writings of Mordechai Lainer of Izbica* (Volume 1); *Radical Kabbalah: The Wisdom of Solomon as the Matrix of the Enlightened Sacred Masculine* (Volume 2) (Integral Publishers, 2012)

humanism, meaning *Spirit Is All*; *I* disappear means *I am Spirit*, too! We take *us* out, because **God is All** and **All is God**.

That could mean that we either emasculate the human being, or it could mean we empower the human being—God is Barbara in person; Barbara is God in person.

Reality/God/Goddess is having a Barbara experience. All of a sudden, we realize that this understanding of a world that's permeated with Spirit creates ahumanism.

Spirit moves uniquely through me:

- With unique cellular code
- With a unique DNA code
- With unique subatomic code
- With unique organization of intimacy
- With muons and hadrons and quarks and leptons

The unique signature of Barbara is not a mistake. The frontal cortex is not a mistake. **Spirit intended unique humans; and Spirit intended us to discover and to disclose that we are evolution in person; and Spirit wanted to reveal itself as us in us and through us—even as She holds us.**

On one hand, we experience prayer, Rumi's *I want to foll into the arms of the Beloved.* The Beloved is holding me in every second.

Yet, in the mystery of Outrageous Love, the mystery of Evolutionary Love, as the Beloved holds Barbara, the Beloved wants Barbara to know:

Barbara, I'm holding you. You don't need to do it all yourself.

If you think you have to do it all yourself, you'll get lost in your arrogance; you don't have to do it all yourself.

I'm holding you in every second, and in paradox of the self-same moment in lived realization.

I'm holding you. I am you. They are both true.

I'm holding you and I am you, non-dual humanism, acosmic humanism; and I realize I'm holding you in love; and My love is incarnate uniquely in you.

The invitation of your life is to be lived as love, but not as just anyone, not as a generic love—but love to be lived as Barbara; love to be lived as Marc; love to be lived as Sally, Lisa, as Chahat, Kristina, Annie, Brett.

In other words, it's a CosmoErotic Universe. **It's a universe driven by desire, and the CosmoErotic Universe awakens as *Homo amor universalis*, in person, unique.**

So, we realize what Barbara and Marc's job is. Our job to start… I don't know, let me make something up…

Are we supposed to start a cosmetics business? I don't think so.

Are we supposed to start a university? Probably not.

Are we supposed to start a network which offers a thousand courses and all sorts of different things; facilitate that network that needs being done in the world—which is a gorgeous thing to do? No.

Our job is to offer our unique gifts in joining genius and manifesting Evolutionary Church together. That's our job.

But at the same time, our job could be something just as equally important, as equally valuable. Our job could be to live in Boise, Idaho and to be the most awesome kindergarten teacher for twenty-five kids every year, and to shape the hearts and minds of those twenty-five kids. That would be just as important. No difference. There's no grandiosity here.

Everybody has a unique gift that they can give towards the healing of the whole story. When I give my unique gift in my unique circle of intimacy and influence, I become powerful again, and all of a sudden, **I realize I don't have to heal everything**.

Actually, for most people the desire to heal everything is a trick of the ego.

Barbara and I cannot heal everything. Even articulating a new source code, we can't heal everything. We need many partners doing many different things, joining together now.

What I'm doing this week is I'm saying *oh the new lineage is Homo amor universalis* the new lineage is like, oh my god, CosmoErotic Humanism, Evolutionary Unique Self, Conscious Evolution. This is the new lineage we are calling it CosmoErotic Universe.

Humanism means we live in a universe which is a love story. We are actors in that love story, and we have unique outrageous evolutionary acts of love. It's Evolutionary Love all the way up and all the way down. And Evolutionary Love awakens and incarnates as us, in person.

Every child that awakens in Reality should awaken and know I *am a unique expression of Evolutionary Love in person* and if **I'm willing to go all the way then I will be healing something in the very source code of Cosmos, because nothing is separate from anything else.**

We now know in systems theory, in chaos theory, whatever I do ripples through the entire system—there is no separation if I'm willing to go the whole way in person.

If I'm willing to go the whole way then I'm *in power.* I'm actually healing. I can open my heart again. I can feel the whole thing . . . because I know that my contribution to feeling the whole thing is healing that which is mine to heal.

I'm willing to go the whole way. Who's willing to step into that? That's our question: am I willing to say *I'm willing to go the whole way*? That's a big thing to say, *this is a big huge commitment. I'm going to take with me whatever I need to take from yesterday.* I'm willing to go the whole way. We need all of us in the symphony.

Feel that part that says *let me watch everybody, but I'm not going to do it—* that's the part of me that's closed down.

> *Am I willing?*

> *I've never written anything before, but I'm ready. I'm saying I'm willing to go the whole way.*

When that happens, when I reach in and I say, *okay I'm not going to watch; I'm going to write this on the lips of the Divine. I'm willing to go the whole way.* Then the gap between our ability to feel the pain and our ability to heal the pain is closed and we can open our hearts and just feel it—I'm willing to go the whole way.

When I'm willing to go the whole way and I write that, literally, my life changes. Blessing starts to flow to me. If you feel like a gap in blessing in your life and you want to open up the springs of blessing. **When I say I'm willing to go the whole way, the Universe reaches toward me. The Universe says, I'm willing to go the whole way *with you*.** If there's a gap, there's a crimp in the flow of blessing. By stepping up and saying I am willing to go the whole way, the universe says, *okay, I'll be your partner— I'm going to go the whole way with you.* Oh my god!

So, our lineage is *we are Evolutionary Love in person*!

THE WHOLE IS REPEATEDLY GREATER THAN THE SUM OF ITS PARTS

I'm taking up on the awesome word *whole as relates to the whole is greater than the sum of its parts.*

But here is a miracle of nature forming whole systems out of separate parts, for billions of years. It's when we can think that each of our bodies has trillions of cells that no engineer in the world could organize into a whole body.

I'm putting forward an awesome thought of a whole planetary body. It is that same tendency in nature to form single cells, multi-cells, and so forth. We as humans are going the whole way when we are putting Evolutionary Love into all the qualities of *Homo amor universalis* including high tech. Many of us feel high tech in-and-of-itself is destructive, but high tech infused with Evolutionary Love—absolutely!

Each of us who is coming in with our wholeness and our whole gift, into a body that nature has a capacity to integrate into something so much greater than the sum of the parts of any whole.

I'm now placing our church in the field of the whole system of a planet which is in either devolutionary cycle or a planet in birth of its next stage. So, place the individual human coming in, and then place the Eros of the total story of evolution in love. We have, here, something as great as Handel's *Messiah* times ten. Oh my god, we have the glory, glory, glory coming from *Mine Eyes Have Seen the Glory.* We are so totally love.

I just want to have a moment of our eyes seeing the glory of *Homo amor universalis* in CosmoErotic Universe, **coming together as a whole so that every one of us then becomes, like an eye can see, and an ear can hear, and a finger can move, because it's part of a whole body being born.**

LET'S BRING IT TOGETHER

What do we call this? We don't call it *Homo universalis.*

We call it *Homo amor universalis,* and *Homo amor universalis* means is that techno-optimism by itself is inadequate.

High tech by itself won't do it. The point of *Homo amor universalis* is:

Only High Tech Used with Evolutionary Love is Going to Take Us the Next Step.

The new whole, the new whole system, we have a name for it here—we call that Unique Self Symphony: A Planetary Awakening in Love through Unique Self Symphonies.

Those words these aren't slogans. Every one of these words means something real. **We realize that through individual uniqueness, that uniqueness doesn't make me separate.**

It's not an individual giving—my uniqueness *connects* me to the Unique Self-symphony. We are invoking, in the church, *Homo amor universalis*. We are investing high tech with Evolutionary Love, and we're coming together as a symphony.

Then we say together, as you say, Beloved Barbara, "our eyes have seen the glory of the coming of the Lord."

Lord both holds us (the God that's beyond us and the God that infuses herself as us) and as we feel that, we are delighted beyond delight.

LET'S MAKE A CONTRIBUTION

I want to just ask everyone to take a second to make a contribution. Let's make a contribution and build this church so we can take this message and move it into the world in the best way we can, because it's actually your contribution that allows this church to go on. I do. Barbara does.

Then, oh my God, we end just looking in each other's eyes.

What a delight, and what an honor to be here.

CHAPTER TEN

EVOLUTION IS ALLUREMENT, DESIRE, AND INTIMACY IN ACTION

Episode 80 — April 28, 2018

I AM EVOLUTION IN PERSON

The code for today is these remarkably beautiful words and to clarify them. Read these words slowly and see what occurs in you. Allurement, go down deep in yourself, **allurement**. Second word: **desire**, third word: **intimacy.**

I am clarified allurement.

I am clarified desire.

I am clarified intimacy.

Evolution is Allurement in action.

Evolution is Desire in Action.

Evolution is Intimacy in Action

Let those beautiful phrases and words sink in. Consider this: I am a member of *Homo amor universalis* feeling allurement. I am a member of *Homo amor universalis* feeling desire. We are the intimacy of evolution in person.

I (Barbara) took a walk early this morning in the beautiful Colorado Springs' sunshine to say we are *Homo amor universalis* feeling allurement. What did I feel from the perspective of being a member of the new species? I had to go right back to the origin of creation. I had to go back to the earliest impulse of the impulse of evolution itself and could feel its allurement. We've been through this; we've said this before.

Particle with particle, cell with cell, and all the way on up, but now, in me I could feel the triumphant impulse of the whole story as me, because none of me would be here without that. That was allurement, attraction, and then comes desire. It has always been longing, this huge, incredible longing in me. So much so, that I've been trying to say, *Stop it Barbara. Don't long for anything anymore. What's wrong with you? Why are you longing, why?*

Because I am evolution in person. I am *Homo amor universalis*. We are that in the church of Evolutionary Love. **We are longing for that greater and greater unfoldment of our essence, and finally, intimacy. We are intimacy. How does that make you feel? There's a bubbling up of joy and then the idea that evolution is desire. Evolution is intimacy in action.**

For a moment, take the deepest possible experience that you could have of being a member of *Homo amor universalis*. Just feel it. That means your spirituality, your vocation, all the innovations in the entire world, all the high-technology, nanotech, biotech, quantum computing, artificial intelligence. All of it is internalized in *Homo amor universalis* as our desires. See if you can get a fragment of the feel of it. It is like internalizing God, and we have said that too: each of us is God in action.

But when you take *Homo amor universalis* personally and internalize these phrases, they bring clarity and incarnation to the new configuration of yourself as this. Here we are joining together in the church of Evolutionary Love to incarnate as the flesh and blood of ourselves, as the heartbeat, as the yearning, as the new species for the first time.

WE ARE TAKING RESPONSIBILITY FOR EVOLUTION

We are *Homo amor universalis*. We are, together, the new human.

We are in Evolutionary Church standing on the abyss of postmodernity, which deconstructed everything. Postmodernity told us that there are no stories and lost the beauty of knowing that we matter ultimately. So the fundamentalists looked at post-Modernity and they said, *Oh, my god, this is horrible and Modernity is even worse. Let's go back to the traditional period, let's go back to the Word of God as it lived in the old sacred texts.*

But that is not what we are saying. We are saying:

> Yes, we love the old sacred texts, and we love that which was good, and true, and beautiful in them. But we don't love the fact that they were homophobic and ethnocentric, that they preached war, that there was not a sense of the profound feminine, that there wasn't a universal sense of human rights. We don't love all that.

We don't want to go backward. **We don't want to be regressive and we are not satisfied with Modernity, with its beautiful vision of progress, because modernity lost touch with the eternal Spirit.**

We are realizing that there are new texts to be written, and the new texts to be written are the texts of evolution itself. Evolutionary spirituality says that the text of the Divine is written in our bodies, and it is written in the evolutionary process, and it is written in our cells, and it is written in our yearnings, in science, and in the great texts.

We are going to take the deepest truths of all of those and weave them together in an evolutionary World Spirituality that steps beyond postmodernity and invites us to a new world. Now, if we think that is a casual endeavor, let's just say it clearly: without that endeavor there probably will not be a tomorrow. The existential threat in the world is so great, and so real, and there are so many different sources.

If we don't articulate a shared vision of value and meaning, a shared language of love that invites us all to tomorrow, for the first time in history we can accurately say there will not be a tomorrow.

That is what we mean when we say that we need a story equal to our power. **Let me add that we need a story *of power* equal to our power. We need a story *of love* equal to our capacity to destroy, which transforms that capacity into a capacity to love unlike any other that ever was, is.** We need to declare ourselves as the new human and as the new humanity. We are generating Evolutionary Love Codes and unfolding them together here at church. Church is not a casual gathering. It is not another form of *wisdotainment*. No, at church we are saying, *we are taking responsibility as da Vinci did in the midst of Modernity with his cohorts in Venice, in Florence.*

We are taking responsibility for evolution. We are participating in the evolution of God.

We are participating in the evolution of love. We are taking responsibility to articulate a new vision, a World Spirituality. We are here, not only for our own delight—and we are delighted—and not only for our own pleasure—and we are pleasured—here in church by the good word of all of us being together; we are here for the pleasure of Reality. Evolution evolved because it feels good, and it *feels* good when it *is* good: it is a clarified feeling of good. **It is a feeling of good that leaves a deep aftertaste.**

Listen to our code and let's feel into it: I am clarified allurement. I'm not just allurement, I'm clarified allurement. I am clarified desire. I am clarified intimacy.

Evolution is intimacy in action. Evolution is allurement in action. Evolution is desire in action.

These are the qualities of what we have declared to be *Homo amor universalis*. Let's take it beyond Christ consciousness. Christ was beautiful, but *how many people died in the name of Christ that cannot believe it all*, said Crosby, Stills, Nash and Young. This is beyond Christ consciousness.

Christ consciousness lived in a world which was ethnocentric, in which the sword of Constantine launched Crusades. **Let's go beyond Christ consciousness. Let's incarnate *Homo amor universalis*: I am allurement.**

What we've done in our modern culture is, we have turned off our allurement. We are afraid, as Barbara says, *Why am I longing so much? I have to stop longing so much, I have to stop*. We are afraid to long deeply, we are afraid to yearn all the way, we are afraid to desire, we've exiled desire.

All that *desire* means these days is a passing sexual desire, and we forget that the *sexual models Eros*. Eros is how we live in every field of our life. Eros was here for billions of years before sex!

I am allurement, I am desire, I am intimacy. And intimacy means shared identity. Intimacy means we are intimate together. Cells come together and create a multicellular identity. Atoms come together and create a molecule. Intimacy means that parts come together and create a new identity, a new whole system identity, greater than the sum of the parts. Intimacy means at its core, shared identity.

We are together in Evolutionary Church as a new shared identity. We come to Evolutionary Church and we feel: I'm not just getting serviced by the church; I am the church. I am the Body of Christ, but Christ the Evolutionary Christ, the Evolutionary Mohammed, the Evolutionary Moses, the Evolutionary Buddha. It is us, our *sangha*.

127

We care for each other madly, we meet each other, and we open our hearts; and we say *let's be allured to each other.* But more than that, let me be allured to fix something in the world that only I can fix. Often, we experience being allured to fix suffering, but then we clamp our hearts down and I say *it is not mine to do.* Maybe I'm allured to adopt a child and send twenty dollars a month for a child in Africa, but then I close my heart and I go on and I write a poem to myself because it is not mine to do. I desire to change something in the world that could only be changed by me, but then I clamp down my desire because I'm told that it is grandiose. It is too grandiose, my therapist says; it is some sort of character problem.

No, let's feel that we *are* grand, let's feel the grandness of our desire, the grandness of our allurement. Our profound desire is to be intimate, not just with myself, not just with the partner who lives with me, or doesn't live with me, or not just with my friend, or not just with the three people around me; I want to be intimate with Reality. **Homo amor universalis is intimate with Reality itself.**

EVOLUTIONARY PRAYER IN THE INTIMATE UNIVERSE

I understand that we live in an Intimate Universe. This is the ground of our prayer. We are going to pray from that place. We ask, intimately, God who is the Infinity of Intimacy. We are here to evolve God. God's not that cosmic vending machine. God's not small, God's not Santa Claus owned by one religion.

God is the Infinity of Intimacy. God is the dance of allurement, all the way up and all the way down. God is incarnate as desire at every level of Reality—desire to traverse the distance and become intimate, desire to feed the hungry, desire to heal the oppressed, desire to be fully creative, fully unique, filled with goodness, truth, and beauty. That's desire. Can you feel that?

People are going to tell us that *it's too much*. People often say, *you're too much*, that Evolutionary Church is too much. No, it's not too much—it's not even barely enough. You are the beauty. *I wish that I could show you when you are lonely or in darkness the astonishing light of your own being,* your own allurement, and I wish that I could show you when you are lonely or in darkness the astounding, gorgeousness of your desire. I wish that I could show you when you are lonely or in darkness the shocking beauty of your intimacy.

Take that realization into prayer. We come before God—and, yes, we use the word God. We don't leave the word God out, because we want to evolve what God means. God is the Infinity of Intimacy. We use the word *church* and we deal with the dissonance of the word. We are not going to call it a collective, and we are not going to call it a communion. **By church, we mean synagogue, and mosque, and collective, and communion, but we use the word Church in order to feel into the pain that word has, to tie into the gorgeousness and the goodness of the lineage, and to clarify all that needs healing in that word called church.** We chose it intentionally.

Church has so much baggage, and often we try to leave our baggage behind. There is another way to engage baggage, which is to transform it. Seventy percent of the world today lives in some form of church, mosque, and synagogue. And seventy percent of that world is living under values that are actually Premodern. Instead of cutting off from it, which is the move of the Human Potential Movement, and instead of calling it a collective, which is the New Age move, what we are saying is that we are going back:

> We are taking the best of premodernity, which is the best of the church, synagogue, and mosque. We take the world's best of modernity, and then the best of postmodernity and then we pour new wine into old flasks.

So, the reason we've chosen the word church is because we know there's baggage. We want to change the vibration and feeling of what church means. We want to uplevel. It is the same reason we use the word God.

The god you don't believe in doesn't exist. We want to participate in the evolution of the church.

We want to get comfortable with being uncomfortable.

We are here to heal church and heal God, because God waits for us to heal Her. That is what creation means: God turns to human beings and says, *I love you madly and I'm going to enter a relationship.* Infinity desires finitude, and we are finitude; and God says, *I love you so madly, but only you can heal.*

PRAYING TO FULFILL OUR COLLECTIVE ALLUREMENTS

Homo amor universalis never has had a church. It has never had a congregation. It has never had this particular moment of evolution when we are told we will either go down quickly toward the devolution of our environment and species or, we are told, we are going to go up quickly to a future equal to Her spiritual, social, scientific, technological, and universal capability. Well, who is going to do that?

> *Let's imagine for the moment that we are at the actual shift point of planet Earth when evolution is right now a question.*

It never has been a collective question for the human species to ask whether or not we will evolve. This church has come into form at the exact moment when this question arose for humanity.

We are *Homo amor universalis* praying for fulfillment of allurement, for everybody's allurement. Let's get inside our allurement as *Homo amor universalis.* I am praying for all the new capacities of humanity to heal everybody who is hungry, everybody who's left out, and everybody who doesn't know they can make it. I am experiencing that, because we are one living body praying as *Homo amor universalis,* and that's my allurement.

What is our desire as *Homo amor universalis?* Let's get in touch with desire at this scale. Mine is the planetary awakening in love through a Unique Self Symphony. It is a birth moment. Isn't it gorgeous to share that desire? We have come together for the birth of *Homo amor universalis* as an opening of those capacities in general. The Unique Self Symphony means everybody on Earth who has a gift to give is giving it, symphonized by the great creative process awakened by the next stage of evolution, which is the God Force in person as us. I desire for humanity to start loving each other. We are in the birthing room, not in the hospital or Hospice.

As *Homo amor universalis,* we are yearning for intimacy—intimacy at this scale. **Intimacy is usually so personal; this intimacy is personal and universal at the same moment**. I want to be intimate with everybody's spiritual impulse of creation. I want to be intimate with everybody's vocation of destiny. They're not just a nice projects. Destiny is the calling within you, and the convergence of all vocations of destiny is the Unique Self Symphony.

Homo amor **is praying for the symphony of vocations of destiny of all peoples of Earth.**

We are *Homo amor universalis* praying for the synergy of all our innovations: new innovations in health, education, economics, science and technology, governance. Everything that is emergent in every field is part of our body.

We are now praying for the unification of our innovative capabilities as humanity in its moment of birth. **We have to expand our capacity for joy to handle this.**

We have only just begun now, because we have not been able to infuse high-tech genius with vocations of destiny. We have not gotten to the folks at Singularity University and everywhere else on Earth where they may be, who are now inventing extended capabilities in every field, and have yet to incorporate this new story of Evolutionary Love. They have invented capabilities and intelligence in high speed travel, and they need to simultaneously invent capabilities in love. They are all turning on now, alongside us, as *Homo amor universalis* at Singularity University. Let's consider it a symbol of the love that's pouring into that high-tech genius.

When we say that intimacy is both personal and universal at the same moment, we are talking about the place where the personal and the universal kiss each other. That's the place where *hitnashéq araa shamayin*[12] in Aramaic, where heaven and earth kiss.

It is when I'm helping someone in my little unique circle of intimacy and influence, and yet I feel like I'm not doing something small, but I'm actually changing everything. When I am doing nanotech and high tech, I'm totally personal and intimate. It is where the personal and the intimate meet and it is where I know that I am intimacy. In other words, it is not only *I want to be intimate*. It is *I am intimacy*. I am allurement.

MEDITATING ON THE BABY OF *HOMO AMOR UNIVERSALIS*

We think of the stories of the birth of the Christ child and how adorable the Christ child was there in Bethlehem. Who would have guessed: there was this little baby and somehow some people knew about it? So, let's say this is like the birth of the *Homo amor universalis*: as there once was a Christ child, there now is a *Homo amor universalis* child.

Let's envision the baby. Let's envision at this very moment, a baby, because the idea of incarnation is that I hold the Christ in the body. If this is the most beautiful baby you have ever seen, it might have been your baby. It might have been your child. It might have been your niece, your nephew,

---

12   *Hitnashéq* means to kiss or embrace. *Araa* means earth. *Shamayin* means heavens. Together, this phrase could mean the earth embraces the heavens or a kiss between earth and heaven, reflecting a union of spiritual and earthly realms

or it might have been a friend's. Envision the baby in this moment and see that baby as *universalis* . This is allurement, intimacy, and desire.

Now step into a meditation for a moment: I am the baby. I am allurement. I am intimacy. I am desire. I am longing, I am the baby long-awaited. Speak it from the Divine lips, to know that God knows: *I've been waiting for the Church of Evolutionary Love, where I am the baby. I am desire, I am allurement.* Stay with it. We are meditating now, we are in the ecstasy of meditation. I am the baby, I am allurement. **We are evolving the source code, and you can't evolve the source code just by saying it.**

Notice that this is the first time this story has ever been told. This particular story of the birth of *Homo amor universalis*, being born as a whole system in recognizing the moment of its own birth within the church. This is an epic drama. If I were Steven Spielberg, I would have this on the biggest screen you've ever seen, because this is drama.

There's nothing more beautiful, more gorgeous, and more dramatic. So, instead of putting up the picture of the baby in the manger, which is also a good idea, we are with the baby right now, we are the wise men and the wise women—it is us. We have the wild privilege of being connected in our deepest Soul Root to come together and say:

> We are standing for evolution, we are evolution awakening as desire, evolution awakening as intimacy, and evolution awakening as allurement.

Let's understand, my friends, this is the best science and the best mysticism. And there's no difference, in depth, between the scientific and the mystical. All mysticism is the expression of exterior science.

When those quarks are allured to each other, they say *quark*. Like ducks quack, quarks quark. They say: *I am desire.* Quarks say, *I am intimacy.* Quarks say, *I am allurement.* When quarks come together and all the process happens, it becomes heavy. **Heavy matter becomes stars, and the stars explode, and those stars live in us. That is allurement, that is desire,**

that is intimacy alive in us. It is the truth. Not to get that I am allurement, I am desire, I am intimacy, is not merely a detail; *that's actually to be insane.* Not to get that, is to not know the nature of Reality.

It is very important when any culture knows how to tell the new story. We have talked about da Vinci. We have talked about the times in Greece. This is one of those times and this is the moment in time to tell such a story ourselves.

APPENDIX: SONGS

THE BATTLE HYMN OF THE REPUBLIC—JULIA WARD HOWE[1]

Mine eyes have seen the glory of the coming of the Lord.

He has trampled down the vintage
 where the grapes of wrath are stored.

He has loosed the fateful lightning
 of his terrible swift sword.

His truth is marching on.

HOW COULD ANYONE—LIBBY RODERICK[2]

How could anyone ever tell you
 you were anything less than beautiful?

How could anyone ever tell you
 you were less than whole?

How could anyone fail to notice
 that your loving is a miracle—
 how deeply you're connected to my soul?

---

1 Julia Ward Howe, "The Battle Hymn of the Republic," 1862.
2 Libby Roderick, "How Could Anyone," on *If You See a Dream* (Turtle Island Records, 1990), CD.

I WANT TO KNOW WHAT LOVE IS—FOREIGNER[3]

I've gotta take a little time,
a little time to think things over.
I better read between the lines,
in case I need it when I'm older.
(Whoa, ooh-ooh, ooh-ooh)

And this mountain, I must climb
feels like the world upon my shoulders,
and through the clouds, I see love shine,
it keeps me warm as life grows colder.

[Pre-Chorus]
In my life, there's been heartache and pain.
I don't know if I can face it again.
Can't stop now, I've travelled so far
to change this lonely life.

[Chorus]
I wanna know what love is.
I want you to show me.
I wanna feel what love is.
I know you can show me.
Oh, oh-oh, oh (ooh)

I'm gonna take a little time,
a little time to look around me.
I've got nowhere left to hide,
it looks like love has finally found me.

[Pre-Chorus]

[Chorus]

[Outro]

(And I wanna feel) I wanna feel what love is

---

3   Foreigner, "I Want To Know What Love Is," recorded November 1984, on *Agent Provocateur*, Atlantic Records, vinyl LP.

137

(And I know) I know you can show me.
Let's talk about love.
(I wanna know what love is) The love that you feel inside.
(I want you to show me) And I'm feelin' so much love.
(I wanna feel what love is) No, you just cannot hide.
(I know you can show me) Yeah.
I wanna know what love is (Let's talk about love).
I want you to show me, I wanna feel.
(I wanna feel what love is) And I know, and I know.
I know you can show me (Yeah).
(I wanna know what love is) (I wanna know)
(I want you to show me) I wanna know, I wanna know, wanna know.
(I wanna feel what love is) (I wanna feel)
(I know you can show me).

HALLELUJAH—LEONARD COHEN[4]

Now, I've heard there was a secret chord
that David played, and it pleased the Lord.
But you don't really care for music, do you?
It goes like this, the fourth, the fifth,
the minor fall, the major lift.
The baffled king composing Hallelujah.

[Chorus]

Hallelujah, Hallelujah,
Hallelujah, Hallelujah.

Your faith was strong, but you needed proof.
You saw her bathing on the roof.
Her beauty and the moonlight overthrew you.
She tied you to a kitchen chair,
she broke your throne, and she cut your hair,
and from your lips she drew the Hallelujah.

---

4 Leonard Cohen, "Hallelujah", *Various Positions*, Columbia Records, 1984, LP.

[Chorus]

You say I took the name in vain,
I don't even know the name,
but if I did, well, really, what's it to you?
There's a blaze of light in every word,
it doesn't matter which you heard,
the holy or the broken Hallelujah.

[Chorus]

I did my best, it wasn't much.
I couldn't feel, so I tried to touch.
I've told the truth, I didn't come to fool you.
And even though it all went wrong,
I'll stand before the Lord of Song
With nothing on my tongue but Hallelujah.

OM NAMAH SHIVAAYA

Om Namah Shivaaya
Shivaaya namaha,
Shivaaya namah om
Shivaaya namaha, namaha Shivaaya
Shambhu Shankara namah Shivaaya,
Girijaa Shankara namah Shivaaya
Arunaachala Shiva namah Shivaaya

*I bow to the soul of all. I bow to my Self. I don't know who I am,
so I bow to you, Shiva, my own true Self. I bow to my teachers
who loved me with love. Who took care of me when I couldn't
take care of myself. I owe everything to them. How can I repay
them? They have everything in the world. Only my love is mine
to give, but in giving I find that it is their love flowing through
me back to the world...I have nothing. I have everything. I want
nothing. Only let it flow to you, my love... sing!*

INDEX

ABOUT THE AUTHORS

Dr. Marc Gafni is a visionary world philosopher and futurist, one of the leading formulators of world spirituality and religion of our time, and a Beloved teacher and public intellectual. He holds his doctorate in philosophy from Oxford University, as well as Orthodox rabbinic ordination. He co-founded the activist think tank, now called the Center for World Philosophy and Religion where he serves as the co-president with Dr. Zachary Stein. He also served with Barbara Marx Hubbard as co-president of the Foundation for Conscious Evolution, which he consented to lead at Barbara's request after her passing.

He is known for his "source code teachings"—including Unique Self theory and the Five Selves, the Amorous Cosmos, a Politics of Evolutionary Love, a Return to Eros, and Digital Intimacy—and has more than twenty books to his name, including the award-winning Your Unique Self, A Return to Eros, and three volumes of Radical Kabbalah.

He teaches on the cutting edge of philosophy in the West, helping to evolve a new "dharma" or meta-theory of Integral meaning that is helping to re-shape key pivoting points in global consciousness and culture, with the aim of participating in the articulation of what Dr. Gafni together with Dr. Stein and colleagues are calling CosmoErotic Humanism.

At the core of CosmoErotic Humanism is what Dr. Gafni and Dr. Stein are calling First Principles and First Values, Anthro-Ontology, and a Universal Grammar of Value. This is the ground of a new shared universe story and a new narrative of identity for the new human and the new humanity. This is what they are calling the emergence from Homo sapiens to Homo Amor. This shared story rooted in First Principles and First Values can then serve as the matrix for a global ethos for a global civilization.

Together with Dr. Stein and Ken Wilber, Gafni is writing a series of seminal books under the collective pseudonym of David J. Temple, which intend to evolve the source code of consciousness and culture in response to the meta-crisis. The first of those books is *First Principles and First Values: Forty-Two Propositions on CosmoErotic Humanism, the Meta-Crisis, and the World to Come.*

Barbara Marx Hubbard (born Barbara Marx; December 22, 1929–April 10, 2019) was an American futurist, author, and public speaker. She is credited with the Wheel of Co-Creation and together with Dr. Gafni, the Wheel of Co-Creation 2.0, as well as the concepts of the Synergy Engine and the "birthing" of humanity.

As co-founder and president of the Foundation for Conscious Evolution and the chair, for the last five years of her life, of the Center for World Philosophy and Religion, she posited that humanity was on the threshold of a quantum leap if newly emergent scientific, social, and spiritual capacities were integrated to address global crises.

She was the author of seven books on social and planetary evolution. In conjunction with the Shift Network, she co-produced the worldwide "Birth 2012" multimedia event. She was also the subject of a biography by author Neale Donald Walsch, *The Mother of Invention: The Legacy of Barbara Marx Hubbard*. Deepak Chopra called her "the voice for conscious evolution."

In 1984, she was symbolically nominated for the vice presidency of the United States. She also co-chaired a number of Soviet-American Citizen Summits, introducing a new concept called SYNCON, to foster synergistic convergence with opposing groups. In addition, she co-founded the World Future Society and the Association for Global New Thought.

Volume 8 — Evolution Is Love in Action

LIST OF EPISODES

www.ingramcontent.com/pod-product-compliance
Lightning Source LLC
La Vergne TN
LVHW011157080426
835508LV00007B/452